Scripta Series in Geography

Series Editors:

Other titles in the series:

North American Urban Patterns

Maurice Yeates
Queen's University, Kingston, Ontario

 V. H. Winston & Sons

 Edward Arnold

Copyright © V. H. Winston & Sons 1980

First published 1980 by
Edward Arnold (Publishers) Ltd.
41 Bedford Square, London WC1B 3DQ
and published simultaneously in the United States of America by Halsted Press, a division of
John Wiley & Sons Inc.

British Library Cataloguing in Publication Data

Yeates, Maurice Henry
    North American urban patterns. – (Scripta series in geography).
    1. Cities and towns – North America – Growth
    I. Title
    301.36'097   HT122

    ISBN 0-7131-6299-6

Library of Congress Cataloging in Publication Data

Yeates, Maurice.
    North American urban patterns.

    (Scripta series in geography)
    "A Halsted Press book."
    Bibliography: p.
    Includes index.
    1. Cities and towns–North America–Growth.
    2. Urban economics–North America.
    I. Title.
    II. Series.
    HT122.Y43 1980 307.7'6 80-17708

    ISBN 0-470-27017-9

Typeset in the United States of America by
Marie Maddalena of V. H. Winston & Sons
Printed in Canada by The Hunter Rose Company Limited, Toronto.

Contents

Preface

This book involves a different perspective from those usually involved with cities and metropolitan areas in North America. There are many texts and articles concerning the internal spatial structure, and the growth (or decline) of urban areas, but there are few that are concerned with the formation of large urban *regions* that consist of many millions of people. Furthermore, there are even fewer studies that are concerned with the formation of large urban regions in the North American urban system as a whole, that is, involving urban development in both the United States and Canada. As a consequence, I have taken a quite unabashedly "continental" point-of-review, though throughout the book there are a number of comparisons that contrast some of the differences in the U.S. and Canadian urban experience. In some instances, particular issues have been selected to illustrate some of the contrasts that have developed.

The purpose of the book is therefore to (1) define the major urban regions of North America; (2) describe the ways in which the pattern of growth among these regions, and the remainder of the continent, has been changing since 1920; (3) sketch some explanations for these changing patterns of urban growth, and the policy implications of these explanations; and (4) examine a *few* of the issues that the different patterns of growth, and the population shifts, appear to create or are creating. The issues that are discussed will not surprise most students of North American urbanism, but the trans-national perspective that is brought to them may offer some different insights. Naturally, the actual issues that have been selected reflect my recent research and public policy experience.

The structure of the book, therefore, reflects the perspective and purposes. The first chapter discusses the concept of the major urban region, and the criteria that can be used to define such regions. The second chapter describes the economic base of the major urban regions, and indicates some of the shifts in population that have occurred both within and between them since 1920. The third chapter examines some of the theories that can be used to "explain" differential growth among the major urban regions, and comments on their respective plausibility. The fourth chapter is concerned with defining some of the issues that arise from different rates of growth, and decline, among and within the major urban regions; while in the fifth chapter there is an extensive discussion of a range of solutions that have been implemented, or are suggested, for resolving some of these issues. The concluding chapter presents some speculative predictions as to the general level of future population growth in each major urban region to the end of the present century, and comments on the general nature of nonmetropolitan growth.

The reader will notice that, throughout the book, there is an attempt to present a variety of perspectives on the particular trends and issues that are discussed. It is, of course, difficult to present such a variety in a few pages, but an attempt has been mde to be as concise and direct as possible. There is, of course, an additional problem with presenting a variety of perspectives, the foremost being a lack of conviction in some of the approaches that I find the least persuasive. For this, one can only apologize and request indulgence, and suggest that any form of writing is really a kind of experiment. In this case the experiment is to learn whether, and how, a variety of perspectives can be presented in a concise, interesting, and logical manner.

A few words of thanks are appropriate. Victor Winston has been a straight-forward editor who has backed up his convictions by transferring a manuscript into printed book form in a short period of time. Helen Phelan exhibited her, by now, customary patience and care in typing the manuscript and preparing the index. Ross Hough prepared the illustrations in the Cartographic Laboratory at Queen's University. Vic Johnston and Debbie Belfie undertook the compilation of information to define the regions and prepared the historical profiles. The manuscript was written during a part of a sabbatical leave in 1978-79, which was supported jointly by Queen's University, and a Canada Council Leave Award and research grant. But, my deepest feelings of gratitude are directed toward my wife, Marilynn, and children, Maurine and Harry, who maintain a sense of humour about my persistent desire to express thoughts on paper.

Maurice Yeates
Queen's University

January, 1980

Chapter 1

Defining the major urban regions of North America

One of the most dramatic developments in North America over the last quarter century has been the growth of large urban regions. Though much of our attention has, quite rightly, been focussed on the immediate and pressing problems arising from the declining population and economic base of the central cities, there has been surprisingly little attention devoted to the issues arising from the growth of these large urban regions. Apart from Gottmann's unique analysis of the emergence of almost continuous urban development between Boston and Washington, D.C.,[1] there have been few other studies of existing or incipient urban developments of this type. This is unfortunate because (1) the population of North America residing in areas that will be defined as major urban regions is increasing, (2) there is a strong relationship between the central cities and the urban regions of which they are a part, and (3) special issues arise as a result of differences in growth between the major urban regions.

This monograph is, as a consequence, designed to promote discussion of urbanism at the macro or major urban region level. Furthermore, it is hoped that some of the obvious definitional, technical, and interpretive problems that occur will promote others to more intensive investigations. At the outset, however, it is necessary to clarify what is meant by "major urban region," indicate the way in which they have been defined for the purpose of this study, and outline briefly each of the regions. The ensuing chapters will be concerned with the growth of the major urban regions, the causes of differential growth patterns, some specific issues arising from macro-urban development, differences in the response to macro-urban development in Canada and the U.S., and the future growth of major urban regions in North America.

1

CONCEPT OF THE "MAJOR URBAN REGION"

The two basic building blocks of urban regions are central cities, which serve as traditional nodes, and the regions which we associated with these central cities, which are referred to as functional nodal regions. Central cities are the historic location of the economic activities and population that gave rise to urban development in a particular area. Today, these old central cities are surrounded by suburban municipalities which, in effect, form part of the city as they reflect stages in the spillover of growth from the central city. They have, however, confined the central city, for the existence of these surburban areas as legal municipalities, each with local governments of their own, provides a series of barriers to physical expansion of the city. In the parts of North America that have been urbanized the longest, such as along the east coast and around the lower Great Lakes, these old central cities have been confined for many decades, and their populations are decreasing as both people and jobs locate or relocate in areas beyond the city. In other parts of North America, such as in the southwest of the U.S. and western Canada, central cities have been legally defined much more extensively in order to prevent confinement by the growth of independent municipal suburban units.

Functional regions are defined in terms of flows, for they are based upon common interlinkages. A hypothetical example can be used to illustrate the concept. Consider the pattern of flows between four municipalities and the rest of the country depicted in Figure 1.1a. The width of the arrows represents the volume of communting traffic moving between the various sub-areas, and a cursory glance at the diagram yields the impression that the volume of flows between municipalities A and B and between C and D are much larger than those between any other set of municipalities, or any specific municipality and the rest of the country. Thus, A and B, and C and D, may be defined as so sufficiently similar and interdependent with respect to their linkages that they form two regions within the four municipality area. As the sub-areas are urban municipalities, A–B and C–D would form functional urban regions.

A special type of functional urban region occurs when the predominant direction of flows is toward one sub-area. Again, consider the hypothetical configuration of municipalities discussed above, but this time regard D as a central city and B, A, and C as suburban municipalities. If the arrows in Figure 1.1b represent volumes of commuting, then the pattern might be regarded as depicting morning journey-to-work patterns, which would reverse in the early evening when workers are going to their homes. The central city, D, is the primary focus of flows, and is also the largest single source of flows spreading to the three municipalities and the rest of the country. A situation of this kind, when one area is the primary destination, and also a major source of flows to all the other areas, results in a functional nodal region, where the outer limits are defined in terms of the volume of flows to the central city.

These two hypothetical examples are useful because although most urban regions in North America are defined as functional nodal regions, the declining importance of central cities in some areas means that urban regions can no longer

a

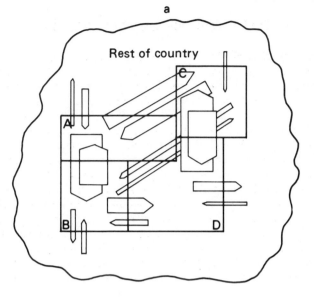

b

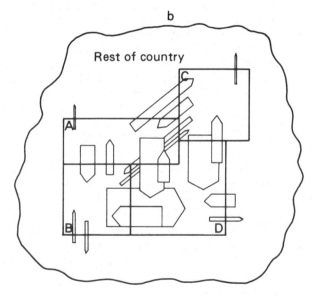

Fig. 1.1. A hypothetical arrangement of four municipalities and the flows between them. The width of
the arrows represents the volume of the flows. (a)
functional urban regions; (b) functional nodal regions.

be defined just in terms of flows to and from the central city. Thus the general case of the functional region, represented in Figure 1.1a, is becoming more and more the basis for amalgamating municipalities that are functionally interlinked. Such regions must now be defined in terms of a complex web of interaction between suburban municipalities. Thus, the simple nodal region has become a more complex multi-nodal space, in which the central city plays a greater or lesser role according to its size and economic importance relative to the rest of the region of which it is a part.

Metropolitan Regions

Central cities and nodal regions can be combined to form metropolitan areas, for, when added together, they give a more realistic impression of the extent of urban development in a particular location. As a consequence, the Standard Metropolitan Statistical Areas (SMSAs) of the U.S. and the Census Metropolitan Areas (CMAs of Canada) are defined in terms of central cities of a certain minimum size and surrounding areas with which they are linked.[2] The physical extent of the interlinked areas are estimated by journey-to-work flows, or commuting patterns. For example, the Syracuse SMSA consists in 1975 of the city of Syracuse (the central city), with the population of 180,000, and the surrounding areas with which it is linked, defined in terms of journey-to-work patterns. The entire region consists of three counties that, when added to the population of Syracuse, result in a metropolitan population of 648,000.

A considerable portion of the population of North America resides in these metropolitan regions. In 1975 there were 135 SMSAs in the U.S., and 13 CMAs in Canada, which contained a population of approximately 250,000 people or more. Together, these large metropolitan regions contain over 63% of the population of North America. We are, therefore, living on a continent in which the dominant frame for human existence is metropolitan in nature. Contrast the two maps of metropolitan North America presented as Figures 1.2 and 1.3. Figure 1.2 indicates the actual location of the larger metropolitan areas (250,000+) on the continent, though not all the metropolises of the east coast and lower Great Lakes are labelled in order to avoid overcrowding in those parts of the map. Figure 1.3 presents in diagrammatic form a transformation of Figure 1.2, in which the area of each state and province is in proportion to its population compared with that of the continent as a whole. Thus Michigan, which had approximately 4% of the population of North America in 1975 is represented on the map with 4% of the "area" of the continent. Within each state and province, the larger SMSAs are also outlined in accordance with the proportion of the population of the continent that they contain. For example, the St. Louis SMSA, with 1% of the population of the continent, is outlined containing 1% of the "area" of the map.

The contrast between these two maps should provide us with some important perceptions concerning the location of the population of the continent. In the first place, the east coast of the U.S., and the area around the lower Great Lakes in both Canada and the U.S., is the location of most of the population of North

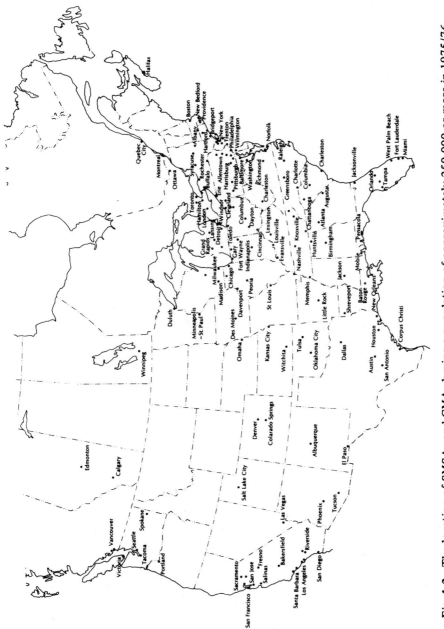

Fig. 1.2. The location of SMSAs and CMAs having a population of approximately 250,000 or more in 1975/76.

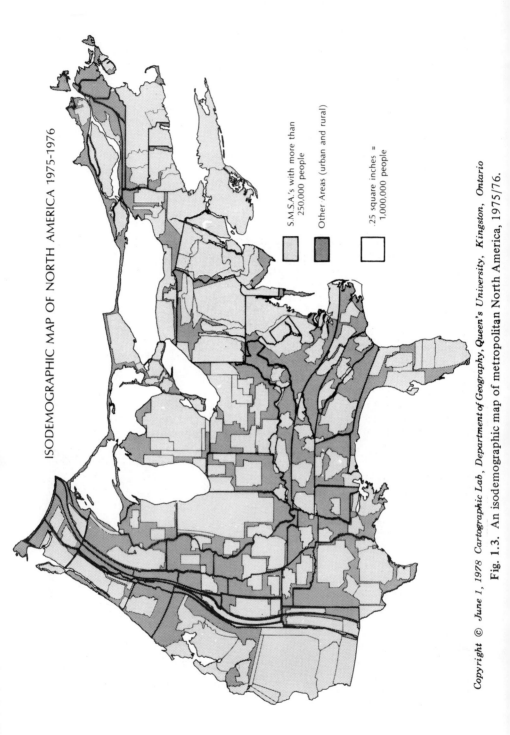

ISODEMOGRAPHIC MAP OF NORTH AMERICA 1975-1976

S.M.S.A.'s with more than
250,000 people

Other Areas (urban and rural)

.25 square inches =
1,000,000 people

Copyright © *June 1, 1978 Cartographic Lab, Department of Geography, Queen's University, Kingston, Ontario*

Fig. 1.3. An isodemographic map of metropolitan North America, 1975/76.

America. This is the "heartland" of the continent, for it is the area from which the continent was settled, and which still contains most of the manufacturing industries. Secondly, within the heartland there are so many metropolises that they frequently become joined and run into each other. This is represented cartographically in Figure 2 by the placement of one SMSA or CMA directly adjoining another. Thirdly, there are other areas of extensive metropolitanism in North America, in particular along the west coast in California, in the northwest around the Puget Sound and Strait of Georgia, along the Gulf coast, and in Florida. These coalescing metropolitan regions form the basis of the concept of the "major urban region."

Major Urban Regions

Major urban regions consist of metropolitan areas that "spill" one into the other. They coalesce either physically or in terms of overlapping functional regions. Physical coalescence occurs when two metropolitan areas have grown so much that the built-up area of one region merges directly into that of another. There are many examples of physical coalescence in North America, ranging from the mammoth Long Island, New York, Jersey City, Newark, Elizabeth strip of major metropolises; the Chicago, Hammond, Gary complex at the southern tip of Lake Michigan; to the complex of municipalities between Los Angeles and San Diego, and around San Francisco Bay. Smaller agglomerations exist in the "Golden Horseshoe" at the eastern end of Lake Ontario, between Dallas and Fort Worth, and the twin cities of Minneapolis–St. Paul.

Coalescence as a result of overlapping functional regions is less evident visually, but just as important in terms of spatial organization. The particular situation being referred to here is not that of overlapping functional regions in cases of physical coalescences, for overlapping is bound to occur in these instances. Rather, the cases of specific interest involve those where the overlapping of functional regions occurs when the physical limits of two or more metropolitan areas are clearly separated. For an example of this type of situation, the commuting fields of the central cities of Cincinnati, Dayton, and Columbus are presented in Figure 1.4. This map of commuting fields has been compiled from separate maps in Berry and Gillard[3] where the contour lines represent the percentage of workers residing in a census unit (such as census tract or minor civil division) employed in the central city of each of the three metropolises. For each metropolis, the 0% line represents the outer limit of commuting to the central city. The contour line representing 30% of the workers employed in the central city is also included, for this usually lies within the formal boundary of the SMSA. The map indicates that even though Columbus and Dayton have not coalesced physically, they have joined one another with respect to their functional regions. In fact the outer limit of commuting to Columbus embraces part of the Dayton SMSA. This overlapping is even more evident in the case of Cincinnati and Dayton, and there is even a small overlap between the outer limits of commuting to the central cities of Columbus and Cincinnati.

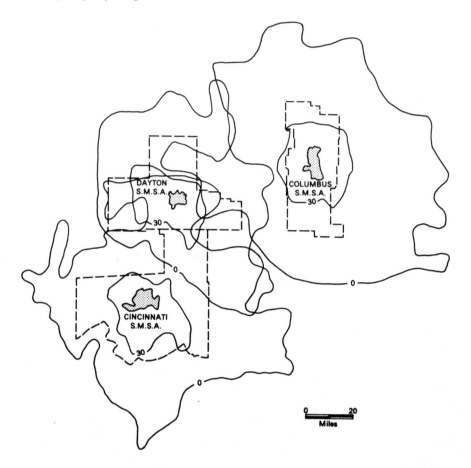

Fig. 1.4. The commuting fields of the central cities of Cincinnati, Dayton, and Columbus, 1970. *Source*: Berry and Gillard, 1977, pp. 220, 230, and 238.

Major urban regions, therefore, consist of a number of metropolitan areas (SMSAs and CMAs) which, because of either physical coalescence or functional overlapping, can be grouped together into contiguous areas of urban development. However, physical coalescence cannot be defined simply in terms of contiguous SMSAs, because in some cases the SMSAs have been defined as such large areas that they embrace extensive areas of agriculture, open land or desert. This is particularly evident in the U.S. where SMSAs have to involve aggregations of whole counties. For example, the SMSA of San Bernardino (40 miles east of Los Angeles) extends to within 30 miles of Las Vegas and includes a large portion of the Mohave Desert and the southern Sierras. As a consequence, the criterion of physical coalescence needs to be defined a little more precisely and used, in some cases, to modify the existence of functional overlapping in areas of low population density.

Context of the Major Urban Region

One of the reasons why it is necessary to undertake an analysis of developing North American urban patterns at the macro or major urban region level is that as the population of the continent becomes more and more urbanized, the difficulty of defining the real physical extent of any one given metropolitan area increases. It may, as a consequence, be useful to place some of the terms that have been used, such as central city and SMSA (or CMA) in perspective with respect to that of "major urban region" and others that are frequently mentioned. The terminology can be discussed with respect to a particular example, that of Atlanta (Table 1.1),

Table 1.1. Some urban concepts related to Atlanta

Terminology	Descriptors	Estimated population, 1975 (in millions)
Atlanta service area	"South" — The Atlanta wholesale and financial service area, bank linkages	21.0
Major urban region	the "urban South" — Population densities, overlapping commuting fields, size	12.7
Georgia	rural vs. urban — Political (state)	4.9
Daily urban system	urban fringe — Daily urban travel	2.1
SMSA	suburbs — Heaviest commuting	1.8
MARTA	central city and inner suburbs — Public transportation	1.0
City of Atlanta	the minority as majority — Political (local)	0.4
CBD	convention hotels, financial and office activities — Business activities	0.003?

as long as it is recognized that the population estimates are specific to one particular case, and that in some other instances the particular descriptors selected may be more appropriate for other criteria.

To the financier in New York City, the conventioner from Moline (Ill.), or the office worker from the outer suburbs, "Atlanta" is a small rectangular area of high-rise modern buildings, located on or adjacent to Peachtree Street in the downtown area. This is the central business district (CBD) of Atlanta,[4] a zone of intensive capital investment over the last 10 years. As with many CBDs in North America, while this area has retained and expanded many of its financial, hotel, and regional office functions, retail activities have tended to decrease. There is, however, a separate part of the central business area, immediately to the south of the cluster of high-rise buildings, which retains many retail activities for the service of the local inner city black population. This, again, is a pattern of CBD finance and retail activities that is found in many North American cities.

The inner city of the metropolis is the city of Atlanta. Although employment in the central city, which includes the CBD, remains reasonably high at over 100,000 workers, the population of the central city has been declining since 1970. At that time the population of the city of Atlanta was almost 500,000, of which a little more than half was black. During the last decade, the out-migration of the white population to the suburbs (which has been a continuing event ever since 1945) has accelerated, and in 1975 the central city contained about 440,000 people, of whom nearly 60% are black. This decline in the population of the central city is also repeated in many North American metropolitan areas, as is the increase in the proportion of the central city population that is black or of some other minority group. In Atlanta, the black population is crowded into the west and central areas of the city, while the white population that remains resides at much lower densities in the northern part of the city. Segregated patterns of these kinds are common throughout North American cities, as is the lower income disadvantaged position of the segregated population.

Somewhat larger in areal extent than the city of Atlanta, and containing some of the suburbs most heavily dependent on employment opportunities in the central city and CBD, is the region to be served by MARTA (Metropolitan Atlanta Rapid Transit Authority). MARTA is constructing, with federal funds, a 53 mile, light-rail, rapid transit system from the higher density suburbs closer to the inner city to the downtown area. The implementation of the rapid transit system in these two counties alone is interesting for it reveals one element of the political difficulties faced by U.S. metropolitan areas in establishing future oriented mass-transit innovations of this type. Only two of the five counties that comprised the Atlanta SMSA in 1970 voted to be included in the MARTA area, the prime objection of the people being that they did not wish to be linked by mass-transit with a predominantly black city of Atlanta. The necessity for local voting for the formation of regional schemes of this type makes the development of metropolitan organization in U.S. cities extremely difficult. The general issue of metropolitan fragmentation will be discussed at greater length in Chapters 4 and 5.

The SMSA of Atlanta consisted of 5 counties in 1970 and 15 counties in the mid-decade census taken in 1975. This increase in number of counties is the result of a recognition that the 1970 SMSA understated the commuting field of Atlanta, and it is also a reflection of the fairly rapid growth of the metropolis between 1970 and 1975. Whereas the city of Atlanta decreased in population by about 60,000 in the 5-year period, the population of the 15 county metropolitan area increased by 210,000 to 1.8 million. The SMSA in effect includes the area of heaviest commuting to the central city, and heaviest between suburb commuting. In general, the outer boundary of the SMSA includes those sub-areas in which 10 to 30% of the workers are employed in the central city.

The boundaries of CMAs and SMSAs are, in effect, continually trying to "catch up" with the outer-boundary of the functional region of the different metropolises. Berry[5] has referred to this functional region as the "daily urban system," and it is defined in most cases as the outer limit of commuting to the central city of concern. In the case of Atlanta, the outer limit of commuting (the 0% contour line), as defined by Berry and Gillard for 1970,[6] has an average radius of about 70 miles from the central city, and consequently embraces most of northern Georgia and part of eastern Alabama. This daily urban system or functional urban region, which can be defined by the outer limit of commuting, is also largely concordant with the "urban field," as discussed earlier by Friedman.[7] The urban field is the location of not only the daily activities of the people inhabiting the metropolis, but the recreational activities as well.

In some instances, the influence of the metropolis, measured in terms of both its functional region and population size, is so great that it dominates the state or province in which it is located. The influence, for example of the New York metropolitan area in the state of New York, or Vancouver in the Province of British Columbia, is so great that the interests and activities of the metropolis are almost contiguous with those of the state itself. In these cases, metropolitan and rural interests are not in balance for urban views predominate. In the case of Atlanta, one of the major issues in the state is the containment of the power of the metropolis in order to maintain some kind of balance in rural-urban interests.

The most extensive region of all pertaining to a metropolis is the area for which it serves as a wholesale, financial, and regional head office center. This is directly related to its position in the hierarchy, which is determined by the number and kinds of service that the metropolis provides, the extent of its hinterland, and the range of its political influence. One concept of the North American urban hierarchy is presented in Figure 1.5, which has been constructed from information concerning correspondent banking linkages between major urban centers in the U.S.,[8] and the location of head offices and major regional bank centers in Canada. The hierarchical structure postulated in Figure 1.5 presents the three highest levels, and combines a fourth and fifth. The lowest levels, which could number another three or four, are not included in the diagram. In this configuration, Atlanta is considered to be a third order center which is directly linked to New York City (which acts as both a first and second order center), and it has an extensive area of correspondent bank linkages via nine fourth and fifth order centers in the south. Thus, in the sense of its position in the hierarchy, Atlanta is a metropolis for most of the "south."

Between its metropolitan position as a service center for the "south" and its

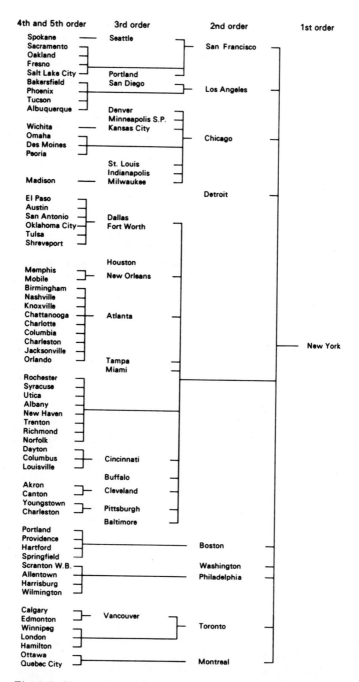

Fig. 1.5. Hierarchical structure of the larger metropolises in the North American urban system.

position as the leading metropolis in the state of Georgia as a result of its extensive daily urban system, is Atlanta's place as part of a developing major urban region through much of the south. The extensive service region, as defined by banking linkages, includes large urban areas separated by extensive areas of agriculture. Atlanta, as we shall learn, is also part of a developing region of almost continuous urbanism.

DEFINING THE MAJOR URBAN REGIONS

One of the most difficult tasks in any form of spatial analysis is defining the geographic extent of the region concerned. The task is difficult because the outer limit of the region cannot be determined by an easily definable line, for it is often a zone of varying width. For example, in the case of the urban regions of Cincinnati, Dayton, and Columbus, the limit of the urban region could well be regarded as the outer limit (0% contour line) of commuting to each central city, but this line is really an interpolation, its position depending upon the interpretive skill of the researcher who drew the line. Furthermore, the location of this outer limit changes throughout the year, usually moving farther from the central city as new residential areas are constructed. But, even though the outer limit of the region is really a zone, there has to be some definite establishment of an outer boundary of the major urban regions, even if this line is a cartographic artifact to be used for statistical purposes.

A British politician is reported to have said that "statistics are like bikini bathing costumes, what they reveal is interesting, but that they conceal is vital." In this case, when the major urban regions are being defined in order to provide some basis for examining changes in rates of growth between the areas, the census units that are selected as the "building block" of the regions are vital. This is because the census units (1) when aggregated define the region and (2) have properties which, by themselves, necessitate a degree of interpretive caution. The census units that have been selected as the "building blocks" for the regions are the counties, for these provide the only readily accessible source of information, in both Canada and the U.S., that can be compared over a number of time periods. When compared with other census units, the boundaries of counties have changed the least over the years, and roughly comparable information has been collected and published at this level of aggregation for a number of decades.

With recognition that the boundaries of the regions are really zones, and that the building blocks of the regions are counties, it is now possible to move to a consideration of the nature of the criteria used to define the major urban regions. Two of the criteria are based on attributes which Wirth[9] considered essential features of urbanization. These are large population size and relatively high population density. It will be recalled that Wirth also considered the impact of population heterogeneity in his rather pessimistic interpretation of the impact of urbanization on social life, but this characteristic is not, at the outset, included in this particular definition of urban regions. A third criterion which is used in the definition of an urban region relates to interaction, defined in terms of journey-to-work patterns, for it is this feature that most clearly represents the dynamic component of inter-action which ties together the sprawling units of the modern metropolis.

Population Density

The chief difficulties with using density as a criterion for urbanization arise from (1) the different sizes of the area units (counties), and (2) the selection of the particular density figure that could be regarded as distinguishing "urban" areas from "rural" areas. With respect to the first of these, consider the case of a county which contains a fairly large urban population and an extensive zone of agriculture. If the county is relatively small in physical size, then the presence of the urban population will be emphasized by the calculation of a fairly high county population density. On the other hand, if the county is large in physical extent, the presence of an urban population may be understated when the population density figure is calculated. Ideally, therefore, counties should be fairly equal in size so that the densities are based on similar possibilities for understating and overstating the degree of urbanism as represented by the density figure. One of the chief difficulties with using counties, or any areal units for that matter, is that they vary in size considerably in North America, with counties in the U.S. generally being larger in the west than the middle-west, south, and east; and counties in Canada generally being larger than those in the U.S. as well as exhibiting a similar east-west variation. As a consequence, the density estimates cannot be used indiscriminately, and must be interpreted in conjunction with impressions gained from the other criteria.

The second consideration is the density that might be regarded as distinguishing "urban" from "rural." This is a difficult question to resolve because there are obviously a vast array of possible "urban" densities, ranging all the way from those representing the inner city, such as Baltimore city, with 10,900 persons per square mile in 1975, to outer-suburban counties, such as Placer County, Ca., with a population density of 64 persons per square mile in 1975. A cumulative distribution of counties according to population density is presented as Figure 1.6, which indicates that whereas about half of the counties in North America have a population density of between 0 and 30 persons per square mile, the other half have a much wider variation from 30 to many thousands per square mile. It would be expected that the range of predominantly "urban" densities would be high. In Figure 1.6, the range in densities appears to begin to increase quite sharply at about the 50 persons per square mile figure.

The selection of the figure of 50 persons per square mile as the density which, on the whole, distinguishes "rural" counties in North America from "urban" counties is reinforced by the detailed empirical work of Russwurm[10] in south-western Ontario. Using much smaller census units than counties, Russwurm developed a fourfold classification of urbanization: (1) urban, areas with a population density of greater than 120 persons per square mile; (2) semi-urban, areas with a population density of 50 to 120 persons per square mile; (3) semi-rural, areas with a population density of 25 to 50 persons per square mile; and (4) rural areas with a popultion density of fewer than 25 persons per square mile.

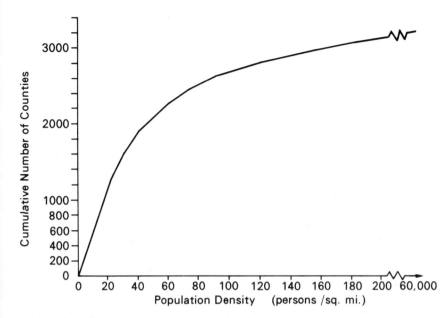

Fig. 1.6. Cumulative distribution of the population density of counties in North America, 1975/76.

Furthermore, Russwurm demonstrates that though many factors mixed in a variety of complex ways may be used to delimit the outer boundary of the urban fringe, a minimum population density of 50 persons per square mile appears to be the best single indicator. Interestingly, Swatridge,[11] following the work of Gottmann,[12] claims that, at the county level of aggregation, population densities of less than 90 persons per square mile are seldom found outside of the *heavily* industrialized urban areas in the northeast portion of the U.S. Thus, the 50 persons per square mile benchmark allows identification of both the high density urban and lower density suburban areas.

A considerable portion of North America has a population density of 50 persons per square mile or more in 1975 (Fig. 1.7) and this portion has increased considerably in physical extent since 1960 (Fig. 1.8). Large areas of contiguous counties with densities above this figure exist along the northeastern seaboard; around the lower Great Lakes and in the Ohio Valley; through a portion of the southern U.S.; along the entire coast and much of inland Florida; in scattered clusters along the Gulf coast; in the southern and central parts of California; and in the northwest of the U.S. extending into southwest British Columbia. Furthermore, there are a few clusters of high density counties around major regional metropolises such as Dallas–Fort Worth, Minneapolis–St. Paul, St. Louis, Kansas City, and Denver. It is interesting to note a few cases where large counties around metropolises, such as those around Phoenix (1.2 million), Edmonton (543,000),

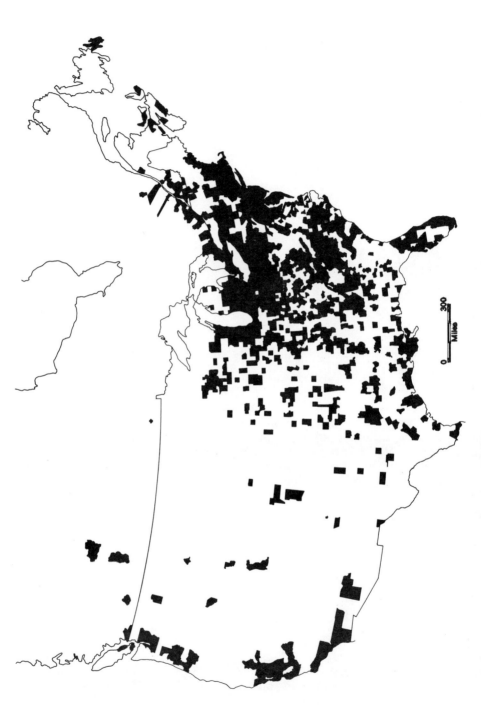

Fig. 1.7 Location of counties with a population density of greater than 50 persons per square mile in 1975/76.

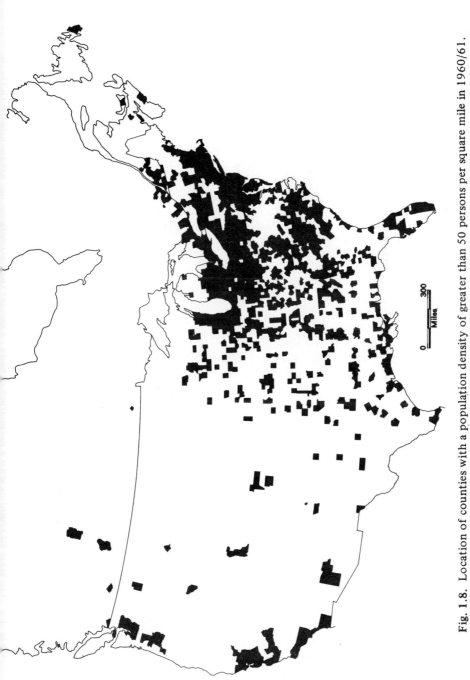

Fig. 1.8. Location of counties with a population density of greater than 50 persons per square mile in 1960/61.

and Calgary (458,000), tend to overestimate the extent of urban development in these areas.

Commuting Fields

In the earlier discussion of the way in which metropolises can merge with others to form major urban regions, it was emphasized that this coalescence can occur as a result of overlapping commuting fields as well as the direct abutment of one metropolis against another. Information, data, and maps concerning the commuting fields of SMSAs and CMAs can be obtained from research reports presented by Simpson and Cromie,[13] and Berry and Gillard.[14] The information, though quite simple, results in the generation of quite complex maps for (as can be realized from Figs. 1.2, 1.3, and 1.4) the large number of metropolitan areas in a few parts of the continent, each having quite a large population, results in a maze of overlapping commuting fields. This is particularly true of the metropolitan areas of the northeastern U.S. and lower Great Lakes, including the area in Canada between Windsor and Quebec City.

Although the many maps presented in these reports are difficult to reproduce, they do provide some important clues concerning the extent of some developing major urban regions. For example, the numerous counties of fairly high population density in California are evidently interlinked by an even more complex pattern of overlapping commuting fields. Somewhat similar in complexity are the overlapping commuting fields that demarcate a zone of almost continuous urbanization and interaction along the Gulf Coast. Rather less complex, but equally as evident, are the commuting fields of the major metropolises extending in the Pacific northwest from Oregon to southern British Columbia. In the southern part of the U.S. a series of adjacent commuting fields extend from Huntsville and Birmingham eastward to Raleigh, S. C.

One important aspect of the commuting fields, and journey-to-work trip lengths, that has been emphasized in both the U.S. and Canadian studies, is the changing nature of the lengths and direction of journey-to-work trips in metropolitan areas. With respect to trip length, it would appear that the average length of the journey-to-work in North America increased by about 10 to 20% in the 1960/1970 period, and the outer limit of the commuting field of most metropolises increased in radius from the central city between 5 and 10 miles. As far as direction is concerned, it is also evident that in the 10-year period there has been a considerable increase in commuting from the central cities to suburban employment zones, a decrease in the comparative volume of commuting from the suburbs to the central cities, and a great increase in the volume of commuting between municipalities and small towns in the outer suburban zones of the larger metropolitan fields.

Size

One of the primary characteristics of major urban regions is that they have a large population size. Although it is difficult to suggest at what stage size becomes an important aspect influencing some of the characteristics of a metropolis, many writers on urbanism have suggested, either through theoretical analyses or empirical observations, that the magnitude of the population and the vastness of metropolitan physical structure do generate certain relationships. On the sociological side, Wirth's observation[15] that the large size, high population density, and ethnic heterogeneity of U.S. metropolitan areas resulted in impersonal, superficial, and transitory social behaviors has been questioned by many writers. Among these, Gans[16] claims that the larger metropolises, with their inner city and suburban areas, provide a variety of environments for living and working, and, as a consequence, are areas in which a variety of life-styles may be pursued.

Economists[17] have long argued that though city size seems to generate problems with respect to congestion, pollution, and city management,[18] the general advantages that occur as a result of economies of scale and greater possibilities for specialization result in higher incomes and a more stable economic performance in the largest places. Thus, on balance, size is considered to be an important component in the creation of higher standards of living. The consequence is, therefore, a continuous drift of population to the largest urban regions, and a steady accumulation of advantages in these areas as a result of investments in infrastructure, service, and productive facilities. While these advantages have been questioned as not being appropriate to developing countries,[19] it is evident that major urban regions are still growing in size in the more developed parts of the world.

The trend toward major urban regions has been codified by Doxiadis[20] in terms of the "science of human settlements," or ekistics. One of the central beliefs in ekistics is that there is an irreversible trend, throughout the world, for the collection of people into larger and more extensive groups of interlinked urban areas. One of the steps along this path of increasing size is the stage of metropolitanism, which, in terms of the ekistics conception, involves metropolises with a population between 800,000 and 5 million. A megalopolitan stage is reached when some metropolises merge, either physically or as a result of overlapping commuting fields, to form elongated linear or curvilinear agglomerations of about 25 million people or more. The ultimate stage is reached when the various megalopolitan areas around the world begin to merge to form ecumenopolis, the universal city. Gottmann[21] has identified six of these megalopolitan urban systems in different parts of the world: the Tokaido Megalopolis extending from Tokyo to Osaka; the Shanghai Megalopolis; the Randstadt of the Netherlands (Amsterdam, Rotterdam); the London Megalopolis extending through Birmingham to Manchester and Leeds; Bosnywash, extending from Boston to Washington, D.C.; and the most extensive of them all, Great Lakes Megalopolis, extending from Chicago to Buffalo and including the area between Windsor and Toronto in Canada.

Size is, therefore, an important criterion in the definition of major urban regions, and though the various size estimates used in ekistics are interesting, there is little empirical or theoretical evidence to support any one particular minimum size. Furthermore, as the estimates of optimum city size (usually calculated on the basis of an examination of the diversity of the costs of government services with population size) vary between 100,000 and 1 million,[22] this body of literature provides limited guidance. One study, however, that is of interest is reported by Yezer and Goldfarb.[23] They use occupation-specific wage levels in large metropolitan areas to estimate the size of a metropolis that is attractive to workers. In their calculations, occupation-specific wage levels are increasingly attractive to workers in metropolises up to a size of 1.5 million, there is some diminution in attractiveness in the size range 1.5 to 3 million, but the attractiveness appears to increase in those metropolitan areas with a population of greater than 3 million. This is probably because metropolises above this size begin to generate large local multipliers as a result of interindustry linkages and the sharing of common infrastructure. As a consequence, it may be useful to regard 3 to 4 million as the lower size limit of major urban regions (i.e., groups of metropolitan areas).

LOCATION OF MAJOR URBAN REGIONS

Given the general criteria discussed in the previous section, nine major urban regions have been defined for North America as of 1975/76. The location of these is indicated in Figure 1.9, and the population, size, and average population densities are listed in Table 1.2. The range in population is quite extensive, from above 44 million in the area between Boston and Washington, D.C. that was originally defined by Gottmann[24] was a megalopolis. Directly adjacent and highly interlinked with this area is the urban region between Milwaukee and Syracuse, which also has a population in the megalopolitan range. This area is, however, more extensive than Bosnywash and has a lower average population density. Closely linked with the lower Great Lakes urban region are the metropolises of the Ohio Valley which have played a significant role in the history of the development of North America. Also closely linked with the lower Great Lakes region are the metropolises of the Windsor–Quebec City urban axis, particularly those located in southern Ontario.

Three major urban regions have been defined as existing in the southern portion of the U.S. These are the Florida and Gulf Shore urban regions, and an extensive area of metropolises and small towns and cities that has been labelled "the urban south." The urban region of Florida consists primarily of a series of metropolitan areas and cities along each coast which coalesce in the central part of the state. The Gulf Shore major urban region has as its major nodes Houston and New Orleans, and though it is discontinuous in terms of population density (Fig. 1.7) there is a high level of inter-county commuting exhibited by overlapping commuting fields. The region of the "urban south" has the lowest population density of the nine regions, and extends from the east coast to northern Alabama. Although each of these regions will be discussed in more detail in the ensuing chapter, the urban south is of particular interest as it consists of a few large metropolises and many small cities and towns which exhibit a similar economic base and are interlinked by much inter-county commuting.

Although the two major urban regions on the west coast appear to be similar in physical size, they are quite different with respect to population size and density. The major urban region of California, which extends from San Diego and the

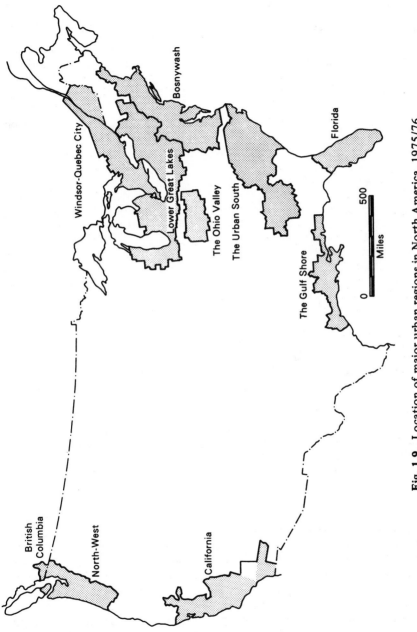

Fig. 1.9. Location of major urban regions in North America, 1975/76.

British Columbia

North-West

California

Windsor-Quebec City

Bosnywash

Lower Great Lakes

The Ohio Valley

The Urban South

Florida

The Gulf Shore

0 500

Miles

Table 1.2. Distribution of population among the major urban regions
of North America, 1975/76.

Major urban region	Population (in thousands)	Size (in thousands of sq. miles)	Density (persons per sq. mile)
Bosnywash	44,384	102.58	432.7
Lower Great Lakes	37,569	128.38	292.6
California	19,668	67.75	290.3
The urban south	12,669	105.39	120.2
Windsor–Quebec City	12,465	67.57	184.5
Florida	7,440	35.96	206.9
The Gulf Shore	6,790	42.69	159.1
Ohio Valley	6,150	19.20	320.3
The Northwest and B.C.	5,734	45.94	124.4
Total of urban regions	152,869	615.46	248.1
Population of U.S. and Canada	235,649		
Percent in urban regions	64.9		

Mexican border in the south to Sacramento in the north, and is contained by the mountain ranges of the Sierras on the east, consists of almost 20 million people. This is clearly an area which has almost grown to the megalopolitan size level, and it is now exerting a political and economic influence over North America similar to that of the lower Great Lakes and Bosnywash urban regions. The major urban region of the Pacific northwest and southwest British Columbia consist of a contiguous set of large commuting regions, and extends some 400 miles between the major metropolises of Portland, Seattle, and Vancouver.

These nine regions together contain nearly 65% of the population of North America. They are not, however, completely overcome by urban development, for each contains a large amount of agricultural land and open space for recreational use. In particular, a large part of the northwest and British Columbia is uninhabited, but the large size of the counties in this area causes them to be included within the major urban region. Also, a number of extensive urban regions that might have been included, such as those around St. Louis, Minneapolis-St. Paul, Dallas-Fort Worth, Denver, and Calgary-Edmonton, have been excluded because either they are not contiguous in terms of the criteria with the regions that have been defined or they do not form regions that are large enough in terms of population size. The nine urban regions are, however, sufficiently varied in terms of their size, economies, metropolitan structure, level of income, past growth, and likely future developments to provide an interesting series of insights into some of the chief issues facing the major urban regions of North America.

NOTES

[1] J. Gottmann, *Megalopolis* (New York: Twentieth Century Fund, 1961).

[2] It should be noted, however, that there is some difference between the U.S. and Canada in the actual details of the definitions. SMSAs include central cities of 50,000 or more plus adjacent counties within a commuting field associated with the central city. CMA's include central cities and adjacent commuting fields, but are not necessarily aggregates of counties. For more detailed definitions see: U.S. Bureau of the Census, *Census of Population, 1970* Vol. 1, "Characteristics of the Population," Section I, Table 5; and Canada, *1971 Census of Canada,* Bulletin 1.1-8, Table 8.

[3] B. J. L. Berry and Q. Gillard, *The Changing Shape of Metropolitan America 1960-70* (Cambridge, Mass.: Ballinger, 1977).

[4] T. A. Hartshorn, *Metropolis in Georgia: Atlanta's Rise as a Major Transaction Center* (Cambridge, Mass.: Ballinger, 1976).

[5] B. J. L. Berry, "The Geography of the United States in the Year 2000," *Transactions of the Institute of British Geographers* No. 51 (1970), pp. 21-54.

[6] B. J. L. Berry and Q. Gillard, op. cit., p. 158.

[7] J. Friedman, "The Urban Field as Human Habitat" in S. P. Snow (ed.), *The Place of Planning* (Auburn, Ala.: Auburn University, 1973).

[8] J. R. Borchert, "America's Changing Metropolitan Regions," *Annals of the AAG*, Vol. 62, No. 2 (1972), pp. 352-373.

[9] L. Wirth, "Urbanism as a Way of Life," *American Journal of Sociology*, No. 44, July (1938), pp. 3-24.

[10] L. H. Russwurm, *Development of an Urban Corridor System: Toronto to Stratford Area 1941-1966* (Toronto: Queen's Printer, 1970).

[11] L. A. Swatridge, *The Bosnywash Megalopolis: A Region of Great Cities* (New York: McGraw-Hill, 1971).

[12] J. Gottmann, op. cit.

[13] J. K. Simpson and M. Cromie, *Where Canadians Work* (Ottawa: Statistics Canada, 1977), No. 99-719.

[14] B. J. L. Berry and Q. Gillard, op. cit.

[15] L. Wirth, op. cit.

[16] H. J. Gans, "Urbanism and Suburbanism as Ways of Life: A Re-evaluation of Definitions" in A. Rose (ed.), *Human Behavior and Social Processes* (Boston: Houghton Mifflin, 1962), pp. 625-648.

[17] W. Alonso, "Metropolis Without Growth," *The Public Interest*, No. 4 (1978), pp. 68-86; and H. W. Richardson, *The Economics of Urban Size* (Lexington: Saxon House/Lexington Books, 1973).

[18] E. S. Mills, "Welfare Aspects of National Policy Toward City Sizes," *Urban Studies*, Vol. 9, No. 1 (1972), pp. 117-128.

[19] A. Gilbert, "The Arguments for Very Large Cities Reconsidered," *Urban Studies*, No. 13 (1976), pp. 27-34.

[20] C. A. Doxiadis, *Emergence and Growth of An Urban Region* (Detroit: Detroit Edison Co. 1970).

[21] J. Gottmann, "Megalopolitan Systems Around the World," *Ekistics*, No. 243 (1976), pp. 109-113.

[22] H. W. Richardson, *The Economics of Urban Size* (Lexington: Saxon House/Lexington Books, 1973).

[23] A. M. J. Yezer and R. S. Goldfarb, "An Indirect Test of Efficient City Sizes," *Journal of Urban Economics*, No. 15 (1978), pp. 46-65.

[24] J. Gottmann, op. cit.

Chapter 2

The major urban regions and changing patterns of growth

The major purpose of this chapter is to describe some of the changes in the distribution of population that have occurred among the major urban regions of North America. These changes take place within the context of the accumulation of capital, for without such accumulation buildings cannot be built, urban infrastructure cannot be constructed, and a continental transport system cannot be developed. Accumulation occurs in a cyclical growth-pause (or stagnation)-growth manner[1] and , although there are frequent upturns and downturns in the economy, the 50-year Kondratieff waves[2] appear most useful in an examination of continent-wide patterns of urban growth. These long waves are identified as corresponding to the mercantile (1780/1840), national industrial (1840/1890), early corporate (1890/1940) and advanced corporate (1940/1990?) eras.[3] As far as the associated forms of urban development are concerned, Walker defines the cities in each of the four stages as "mercantile," "classic industrial," "metropolitan," and "suburban" or "megalopolitan."[4]

It is, however, more useful in the actual examination of the urbanization events associated with each of these general stages of accumulation to define the eras with respect to the mid-points of the Kondratieff waves of accumulation. This is because the product of the investments and the type of urban development that are occurring become quite clear at this mid-point. Furthermore, the mid-point of each of the long waves is usually a period when capital investment is beginning to reach a maximum. Thus, Borchert[5] defines the major stages of urbanization in the U.S. as 1830/1870, 1870/1920, 1920/1970, and focusses particularly on the impact of the transport investments that occurred. These investments are, however, made possible by the amounts of capital that have been accumulating in the two previous decades. Furthermore, the types of urban development that occurred are the consequences of the form of urbanization most suited to that particular stage in the organization of economic activity.

25

The examination of change in the distribution of population among the major urban regions is set in the context of the 1920/1975 period. Thus, the date should reflect the general patterns of change that occurred during Walker's "metropolitan," and that are occurring during his "suburban" or "megalopolitan" eras. In terms of Borchert's transportation-based definition, the time-frame allows us to focus on the distribution of population consequent to the "age of the steel rail" (1870/1920) and that arising from the "automobile era" (1920/1970). In the context of both sets of divisions, the period since 1970 is of particular interest because the events that seem to be occurring should indicate the general pattern of urban development that will continue through, and will, perhaps, be dominant at the turn of the century. But, before commencing a direct discussion of the changes, a brief outline of the urban structure and economic base of each of the major urban regions is in order.

ECONOMIC BASE OF THE MAJOR URBAN REGIONS

Although the location of the major urban regions has been outlined in one or two sentences in the previous chapter, it is appropriate at this juncture to present some brief vignettes of each of the major urban regions. It is quite apparent from Table 2.1 that they differ quite considerably in population size, physical extent, and general density of urban development. They also differ quite considerably in the range of metropolitan development, general age of the cities, and the type of economic base found within each region. This latter aspect is of particular importance because it refers to that portion of the goods and services produced within a region that is sold beyond its borders. The more goods and services a

Table 2.1. Population of the major urban regions at each time period between 1920/21 and 1975/76.

Major urban region	1920/21	1930/31	1940/41	1950/51	1960/61	1970/71	1975/76
Bosnywash	23.27	27.31	28.81	32.62	38.10	43.34	44.38
Lower Great Lakes	19.99	24.25	25.29	28.76	33.98	37.25	37.57
California	3.81	5.22	6.36	9.83	14.62	18.62	19.68
The urban south	6.41	7.35	8.10	9.34	10.59	11.99	12.67
Windsor–Quebec City	4.60	5.42	5.97	7.28	9.73	11.92	12.46
Florida	0.64	1.11	1.48	2.26	4.21	6.00	7.44
The Gulf Shore	1.97	2.46	2.80	3.86	5.20	6.25	6.79
Ohio Valley	3.05	3.41	3.62	4.27	5.29	6.00	6.15
The Northwest and B.C.	1.79	2.20	2.53	3.52	4.39	5.40	5.73
Total	65.53	78.73	84.96	101.74	126.11	146.77	152.87
U.S. and Canada	114.50	133.15	143.28	165.34	197.63	224.87	235.65

region can produce and sell beyond its immediate environs, the more viable it becomes and the more additional wealth (and perhaps growth) will be generated.

Bosnywash

The area that has been defined as Bosnywash in Figure 1.9 is nearly twice as large as that defined as "megalopolis" by Gottmann in 1961.[6] This increase in size reflects the quite considerable growth in population that has occurred within the commuting fields of the metropolises and cities within the region. Gottmann's original definition of the area was based primarily on data pertaining to the 1950s, and the population of the area has increased considerably since that time.[7] Even using the major urban region definition in Figure 1.9, the population of the area has increased by 36% since 1950 and by more than 16% since 1960 (Table 2.1). Today, the population of the region is in excess of that occurring in all but 18 independent countries in the world, and the per capita income of the area is close to being the highest of any country in the world.

The urban region extends some 700 miles from Portland (with an SMSA population of almost 230,000) to Norfolk (Table 2.2), and averages 100 to 150 miles in width (Fig. 2.1). Although the region exhibited quite rapid population growth between 1950 and 1960, growth since 1970 has been considerably less. This is expressed quite dramatically in the recent growth performances of the 17 largest SMSAs in the region (Table 2.2). Whereas these metropolises were the location of 81.5% of the region's population in 1970, by 1975 they housed only 80.1%. Furthermore, three of the SMSAs with a population in excess of one million actually declined in population. Although this may be an indication that the growth of these metropolises had decentralized beyond the immediate SMSA boundaries, nevertheless this experience of decline in SMSA population is a recent phenomenon in North American urban development. The underbounding situation is particularly noticeable in the case of the New York City metropolitan area, where the growth of adjacent SMSAs is almost equal to the decrease in the New York metropolitan population.

The economic base of different parts of the region is summarized in Table 2.3. The data in this table relates to economic areas, as defined by the Office of Business Economics of the U.S. Department of Commerce in 1969, which are based on the commuting regions of major metropolises and formed by combining SMSAs and counties. For example, the economic region relating to the New York City area consists of the New York City, Jersey City, Paterson–Clifton–Passaic, Newark, and Bridgeport–Stamford–Norwalk–Danbury SMSAs. Although some of these areas are rather large, the data in Table 2.3, which represent the percentage of earnings in an economic region that are derived from basic activities, do provide a consistent set of information for the U.S. Thus, for the Boston economic region, 36.8% of the earnings received by employed persons in the economic region is considered to be derived from basic activities. Consequently, 63.17% of the earnings in the region can be considered to be derived from nonbasic activities. Agriculture contributes 0.71% of the earnings in the basic component, mining 0.06%, manufacturing 29.32%, employment in federal government activities 2.39%,

Table 2.2. Population of the larger SMSAs in the Bosnywash major urban region.

Figure ref.	SMSA	1975	1970
N.Y.	New York	9,635	9,973
Phil.	Philadelphia	4,797	4,824
Bost.	Boston-Lowell-Brockton-Lawrence-Haverhill	3,915	3,849
Wash.	Washington, D.C.	3,016	2,910
N-S	Nassau-Sufflok	2,622	2,556
Balt.	Baltimore	2,137	2,071
New.	Newark	1,996	2,057
H.	Hartford-New Britain-Bristol	1,060	1,035
P.	Providence-Warwick-Pawtucket	851	855
B.	Bridgeport-Stamford-Norwalk-Danbury	974	793
N.H.	New Haven-West Haven-Waterbury-Meriden	761	745
W.	Worcester-Fitchburg-Leominster	648	637
ABE	Allentown-Bethlehem-Easton	622	594
N.B.	New Brunswick-Perth Amboy-Sayreville	590	584
J.	Jersey City	583	607
Rich.	Richmond	582	547
	Total	33,562	35,370

Source: U.S. Bureau of the Census, *Estimates of the Population of Counties and Metropolitan Areas, 1975*, Washington, D.C.: U.S. Department of Commerce.

and other activities 4.34%. Although there is some considerable discussion as to the precise applicability of the economic base approach,[8] it does provide a useful descriptive device for discussing the chief economic functions of the major regions.

In the Bosnywash major urban region, it is apparent that the chief basic activity in all but two of the economic regions is manufacturing. Manufacturing is almost the only basic activity in the economies of the Portland, Hartford-Providence, and Philadelphia economic regions; and is the prime basic activity in the New York, Boston, Baltimore, and Richmond economic regions. This concentration on manufacturing is not surprising because the Bosnywash area was the first location in which industrial activity of this type was established in the U.S. While there has been a considerable spread of manufacturing throughout the rest of the continent, the region has remained prominent in the manufacture of food, telecommunication components, clothing, printed products, chemicals, steel, and in the refining of different raw materials.

A second prominent basic activity in two of the regions is employment in jobs funded by the federal government. This is particularly evident in the cases of Washington, D.C., home of the federal bureaucracy, and Norfolk, a major naval establishment. Baltimore and Richmond also have considerable employment in federal-related activities. The third most important general area of basic activities is the "other" category. This component is most noticeable in the case of New

York, and also Boston and Washington, D.C. For the most part, this category relates in these economic areas to the considerable portion of basic earnings which is derived from employment in financial and office activities which serve the continent (and world) beyond the region. In the case of New York, for example, these include the major financial institutions as well as headquarter offices, and as the 11.38% relates to the basic earnings supporting a total population of over 18 million, the number of workers involved is quite considerable.

One element of the basic activity of each of the major urban regions that cannot be ignored is the earnings derived from agriculture. On the average, in the U.S. as a whole, only 10% of the land area in an SMSA is devoted to urban uses.[9] The

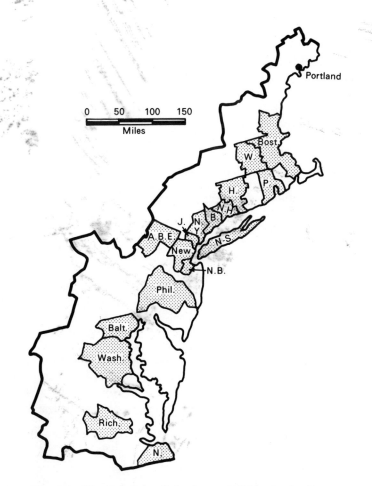

Fig. 2.1. The location of the larger SMSAs in the Bosnywash major urban region.

Table 2.3. Economic base of the economic areas in the Bosnywash
major urban region.

Economic area	1970 pop.	Agric.	Mining	Mfg.	Fed + Govt.	Other	Total
New York	18,228	0.38	0.12	24.65	0.66	11.38	37.19
Philadelphia	7,281	1.12	0.26	32.61	2.20		36.19
Boston	6,338	0.71	0.06	29.32	2.39	4.34	36.83
Washington, D.C.	3,090	0.77	0.14	2.05	32.08	6.13	41.17
Baltimore	2,670	2.49	0.05	24.04	9.64		36.22
Hartford–Providence	2,966	1.20	0.10	39.92	1.71	0.93	43.86
Norfolk	1,232	2.71	0.02	12.84	35.72		51.29
Richmond	1,004	3.33	0.20	21.23	7.93	2.94	35.63
Portland	740	2.76	0.06	33.58	2.32		38.72

Source: Berry and Kasarda (1977), pp. 290 and 296.

rest is devoted to woodland (32%), cropland (24%), pastureland (19%), and other uses. Although in the northeastern part of the U.S. the proportion of land occupied by urban uses is twice that of the average SMSA (19%), there is still a considerable proportion of land in the average northeastern SMSA devoted to forests and woodland (47%) and cropland (22%). Thus, agriculture is an important activity in each urban region, and in the Bosnywash area accounts for over 2% of the basic activity earnings in the Baltimore, Norfolk, and Richmond economic areas.

Lower Great Lakes Urban Region

The lower Great Lakes urban region extends 800 miles from the Milwaukee SMSA on Lake Michigan through to Albany in the state of New York (Fig. 2.2). In 1975 it consisted of four coalescing super-metropolitan areas of continuous macadam and concrete: (1) Milwaukee-Chicago-Gary (about 10 m. people); (2) Flint-Detroit-Toledo (6 m. people); (3) Cleveland-Akron-Youngstown-Pittsburgh (6 m. people); and (4) Buffalo-Rochester-Syracuse-Albany (5 m. people). Although the eastern boundary of the region is defined at Albany, close to the eastern end of the historic Erie Canal, the southern boundary of the region is more difficult to determine. The southern limit has been kept as close to the Great Lakes as the population density and commuting information allows, and has also been influenced by the necessary inclusion of Pittsburgh into the Cleveland complex. These two metropolises grew in tandem during the period of heavy industrialization at the turn of the century and there is now almost continuous urban development along the transport routes connecting Pittsburgh with Cleveland and Lake Erie. The Great Lakes form the common link which has led to the steady convergence of these four super-metropolitan clusters. Although the portion of goods carried on the Lakes today is quite low compared with that carried by truck and rail, the transport routes for these

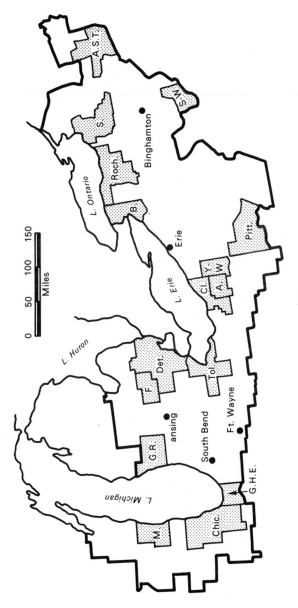

Fig. 2.2 Location of the larger SMSAs in the lower Great Lakes urban region.

31

facilities also follows the edge of the Lakes Ontario and Erie, and from Detroit-Toledo across to Gary around the southern extension of Lake Michigan.

Although the population of the urban region is continuing to grow, it is evident (Table 2.1) that the periods of greatest absolute growth occurred between 1920 and 1930, and 1950 and 1960. The economy of the region is linked most directly with the automobile, iron and steel, and petrochemical industries, and all the myriad activities associated with these. As a consequence, it is not surprising that during the recovery periods following the world wars, when spending on automobiles and other consumer products was particularly high, the region experienced its greatest expansion in population. But, in recent years, the 16 major SMSAs (those with a population greater than 500,000) have, in total, increased in population hardly at all (Table 2.4), and 4 actually declined. This limited population growth does not, however, mean that the four clusters of metropolises will not continue to converge, for the population of these areas, and the manufacturing industries, are continuing to decentralize and thus generate urban expansion.

The dependence of the entire area on manufacturing as the chief component of its economic base is indicated in Table 2.5. The metropolises of the Great Lakes urban region are even more dependent on manufacturing than those located in the Bosnywash area, for all except two of the economic areas have basic earnings of 30% or more from manufacturing. Although manufacturing in the area is quite

Table 2.4. Population (in thousands) of the larger SMSAs in the lower Great Lakes urban region.

Figure ref.	SMSA	1975	1970
Chic.	Chicago	6,983	6,978
Det.	Detroit	4,445	4,435
Pitt.	Pittsburgh	2,316	2,401
Cl.	Cleveland	1,975	2,064
M.	Milwaukee	1,426	1,404
B.	Buffalo	1,327	1,349
Roch.	Rochester	971	962
AST	Albany-Schenectady-Troy	799	778
Tol.	Toledo	781	763
A.	Akron	668	679
S.	Syracuse	648	637
GHE	Gary-Hammond-East Chicago	640	633
S-W	Scranton-Wilkes Barre	637	621
G.R.	Grand Rapids	566	539
Y-W	Youngstown-Warren	549	537
F.	Flint	520	508
	Total	25,251	25,288

Table 2.5. Economic base of the economic areas in the lower Great Lakes urban region.

Economic area	1970 Pop.	Agric.	Mining	Mfg.	Fed. + Govt.	Other	Total
Chicago	8,193	1.09	0.27	32.12	0.99	4.04	38.51
Detroit	5,207	0.48	0.09	42.94	0.39	0.17	44.07
Pittsburgh	3,716	0.79	2.87	36.53	0.45	2.87	43.51
Cleveland	4,255	1.12	0.39	41.70	0.37	0.67	44.25
Milwaukee	2,066	2.28	0.15	39.58	0.47	0.23	42.71
Buffalo	1,642	2.10	0.35	37.36	1.76	0.45	42.02
Rochester	1,016	2.88	0.23	44.14	0.30		47.55
Albany	1,331	1.96	0.45	27.60	8.01	1.85	39.87
Toledo	1,054	4.22	1.00	36.14	0.40	1.04	42.80
Syracuse	1,444	3.38	0.52	29.47	5.68	1.58	40.63
Wilkes-Barre	692	1.60	1.91	33.77	0.53	1.44	39.25
Grand Rapids	1.166	3.33	0.17	38.85	0.42	0.44	43.21
Youngstown	770	0.96	0.42	50.46	0.41	0.60	52.85
Lansing	986	2.95	0.15	38.15	4.95	0.42	46.62
South Bend	747	3.86	0.09	45.11	0.36		49.42
Binghampton	765	4.32	0.12	39.77	3.17	0.51	47.89

Source: Berry and Kasarda (1977), pp. 290–293, 296–299.

diverse, there is particular emphasis on "heavy" manufacturing as opposed to "light." Heavy industries are those that use large quantities of raw materials, often with a considerable weight-loss in the process of manufacturing, and that generate products which are frequently used as input into other manufacturing industries. Examples are iron and steel (Cleveland, Buffalo, Gary, Chicago, Pittsburgh), petrochemicals (Chicago, Cleveland, Detroit), and automobile manufacturing (Detroit, Toledo). Examples of "light" industries are those concerned with electronics, component assembly (such as dishwasher assembly), and printing and publishing. The "heavy" industries are those particularly associated with the emission of pollutants, either in the form of particle emissions to the atmosphere, or water pollution as a result of its direct use in the manufacturing process or as a coolant. General atmospheric and water pollution from heavy industry are of widespread concern throughout the lower Great Lakes urban region.[10]

Although there are only a few metropolitan areas in which there are significant nonmanufacturing sources of basic income, these are particularly important in the Chicago, Albany, Syracuse and Lansing metropolitan areas. Chicago, as the second metropolis on the continent (after New York City), is the location of a large number of headquarter offices and major financial institutions.[11] Hence, the basic earnings of 4% in the "other" category. Albany and Lansing, as state capitals, have a large component of their basic activities in the federal and government employment category, and the Syracuse economic region contains a few defense establishments. A number of the economic areas are quite large and contain extensive agricultural activities, as is indicated by basic earnings of 2% or more from agriculture in 10 of the regions.

California Urban Region

The California urban region provides an interesting set of contrasts with the recent growth performances and economic base of both the regions discussed previously. In the first place, in terms of macro-urban structure, the region has clearly developed around two clusters of metropolises, a northern group focussed on San Francisco and a southern cluster around Los Angeles (Fig. 2.2). Connecting these two areas is a rich agricultural valley in which the SMSAs of Bakersfield (344,000) and Fresno (445,000) act as regional centers. The intensity of agricultural production in this irrigated valley is so great that many food processing and packing concerns have located here and provide a large number of nonagricultural jobs in the service towns.[12] Thus, urban development occurs in a "beads-along-a-string" fashion on either side of highway 99, the original route connecting the northern and southern portions of the state.

A second major contrast with the lower Great Lakes and Bosnywash urban regions is with respect to recent population growth within the urban region (Table 2.1). Whereas the population of Bosnywash grew by 2.4% and the lower Great Lakes by less than 1% between 1970 and 1975, the California urban region grew by 5.7% in the 5-year period (Table 2.6). Furthermore, the population growth of the larger SMSAs, except for Los Angeles, exceeded this rate of growth. There has clearly been a decentralization of growth from Los Angeles to the neighboring,

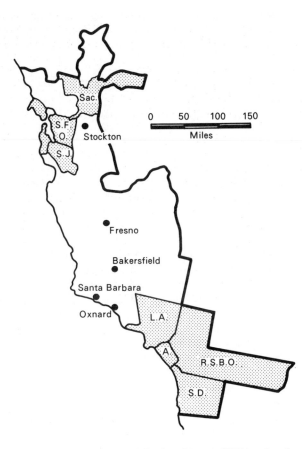

Fig. 2.3. Location of the larger SMSAs in the California urban region.

and contiguous, SMSAs involving Anaheim, Riverside, and Oxnard, with urban development now almost continuous along the coast from Santa Barbara to San Diego, and spreading inland across the desert. Similarly, although urban growth appears to be quite limited in the San Francisco-Oakland SMSA, the growth of the San Jose and Sacramento SMSAs in the 5-year period has been quite dramatic.

The third contrast is with respect to the economic base of the region (Table 2.7). Although the economic regions that are defined for this part of the U.S. are rather large, the indicators of the sources of basic income give a reasonable idea of the economic base of the California urban region. Compared with the Bosnywash and lower Great Lakes urban region, there is far less emphasis on manufacturing. The area that has the greatest emphasis on manufacturing is Los Angeles, which

Table 2.6. Population of the larger SMSAs in the California
urban region.

SMSA	1975	1970
Los Angeles–Long Beach	6,945	7,042
San Francisco–Oakland	3,129	3,107
Anaheim–Santa Ana–Garden Grove	1,710	1,421
San Diego	1,588	1,358
Riverside–San Bernardino–Ontario	1,223	1,141
San Jose	1,173	1,065
Sacramento	880	804
Total	16,648	15,938

has a wide variety of industries ranging from petroleum refining through to aero-space, electronics, and a vast array of consumer-oriented activities. The economic regions of San Diego and Sacramento, which involve the fastest growing large metropolises in the area between 1970 and 1975, have received a large proportion of their basic income from federal and state government sources. San Diego has huge naval defense operations and an extraordinarily large military retirement community, and Sacramento is the capital of the largest state in the Union. The economic area of Stockton probably has the most diversified economic base of any analyzed thus far, with basic income generated from high-value truck farming, light manufacturing, and federal sources (air force defense establishment).

San Francisco serves two functions that provide considerable basic income, apart from that received from manufacturing which is associated mostly with the port of Oakland. In the first place the "city" serves as the western regional headquarters for many federal government departments. Secondly, it is the location of numerous headquarter offices and regional offices, for business serving

Table 2.7. Economic base of the economic areas in the California
urban region.

Economic area	1970 Pop.	Agric.	Mining	Mfg.	Fed. + Govt.	Other	Total
Los Angeles	10,436	1.54	0.58	27.91	1.99	4.34	36.36
San Francisco	5,090	1.96	0.23	17.19	7.97	5.42	32.77
San Diego	1,357	1.56	0.12	14.97	26.59	0.96	44.20
Sacramento	1,089	4.57	0.17	8.23	22.36	3.01	38.34
Stockton	643	13.22	0.27	14.55	11.01	0.68	39.73

Source: Berry and Kasarda (1977), pp. 290–293, 296–302.

California, the west, and dealing with the Pacific trade. Los Angeles also has a significant portion of its basic income derived from financial activities and headquarter offices and their subsidiaries. It also derives some basic income from trade links across the Pacific and to Europe via the Panama Canal.

The Urban South

Although the area that has been defined as the "urban south" (Fig. 2.4) did not grow as fast as the population of North America as a whole between 1920 and 1970, there has been a considerable increase in population during the 1970s. In fact, the rate of population gorwth in the urban south between 1970 and 1975 has been exactly the same as that for the California urban region during the 1970/75 period (Table 2.1), and there is little doubt that the region will be one of the faster growing areas of the continent during the next few decades. The south as a whole (south of the Mason-Dixon Line plus Texas) has experienced a remarkable shift in migration patterns since 1970, changing from being a region of small positive net immigration during the 1960s to large positive net immigration during the 1970s. In fact, this region has now replaced the west as being the recipient of the largest volume of interregional migrants on the continent.[13] Thus, the urban south is of particular interest because it has joined the group of urban areas in the "sun-belt" experiencing relatively high rates of growth as a result of interregional shifts in employment and population.

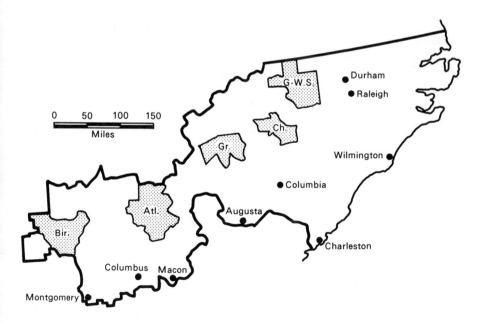

Fig. 2.4. Location of the larger SMSAs in the urban South region.

The urban south is also of particular interest because it has developed along a unique geographic axis: the piedmont of the Appalachians. The rivers and streams crossing the piedmont from the Blue Ridge Mountains to the west and north, before meandering across the coastal plain to the Atlantic, have traditionally provided a location for small manufacturing concerns and towns and cities. Today this geographical feature is demarcated by the long corridor of metropolises from Durham and Raleigh, through Greensboro-Winston Salem, to Atlanta, and extending in transport corridors from Atlanta to Birmingham and Montgomery. The northern edge of this metropolitan corridor is defined by the Blue Ridge and Smoky Mountains, and the southern edge by the extensive agricultural lands on the black earths of the deep south.

An interesting feature of this metropolitan corridor is that the urban areas located within it have grown at a rate faster than the nonmetropolitan areas lying beyond the corridor within the region (Table 2.8). This is in contrast to one of the important growth features identified by Wheat,[14] for the nonmetropolitan areas of the south as a whole have grown faster than the metropolitan areas. Metropolitan growth in this corridor is perhaps related to the excellent set of interstate highway and rail transport links with Bosnywash, which provide a high level of accessibility to this large concentrated consumer market. The effect of the high level of interlinkage is seen most clearly in the economic bases of Greensboro, Charlotte, Greenville, and Atlanta, which have become leading centers for the production of furniture and textiles (Table 2.9). Birmingham, with its unique local combination of coal and iron ore, has traditionally been the heavy industry center of the south.

Apart from the importance of manufacturing in the cities of the metropolitan corridor, and the relatively widespread distribution of manufacturing among the smaller towns and cities of the urban south, 7 of the 12 economic areas listed in Table 2.9 have a relatively large proportion of their economic bases supported by federal and state government expenditures. Expenditures by the federal government for defense establishments have been particularly large in this part of the south (due to the power of southern senators on defense appropriation committees), a situation that has prompted Senator Moynihan (New York state) to remark

Table 2.8. Population (in thousands) of the larger SMSAs
in the urban South region.

Figure ref.	SMSA	1975	1970
Atl.	Atlanta	1,806	1,596
Bir.	Birmingham	793	767
G-W.S.	Greensboro-Winston Salem	765	724
Ch.	Charlotte-Gastonia	595	558
Gr.	Greenville-Spartanburg	526	473
	Total	4,485	4,118

Table 2.9. Economic base of the economic areas in the urban South region.

Economic area	1970 Pop.	Agric.	Mining	Mfg.	Fed. + Govt.	Other	Total
Atlanta	2,296	1.55	0.29	24.05	1.89	8.42	36.20
Birmingham	1,660	4.27	1.51	30.29	3.34	1.12	40.53
Greensboro	1,142	3.49	0.17	42.12	0.75	1.94	48.47
Charlotte	1,489	2.06	0.17	40.56	0.63	1.75	45.17
Greenville	817	1.45	0.14	46.84	0.83		49.26
Raleigh	1,621	12.99	0.31	18.07	13.72		45.09
Charleston	430	3.69	0.03	12.98	34.16	0.30	51.16
Columbia	610	5.63	0.24	18.36	16.29		40.52
Columbus	488	3.17	0.12	22.24	27.20		52.73
Montgomery	686	6.96	0.19	19.00	16.27	0.04	42.46
Macon	496	11.90	1.98	18.20	16.63		48.71
Augusta	461	6.20	0.41	26.54	22.77		55.92

Source: Berry and Kasarda (1977), pp. 290–293, 296–302.

that "our armed forces are clearly preparing to fight the next war in Nicaragua, or at least some place where it never freezes." A large portion of the economic base of the areas beyond the metropolitan corridor is also derived from agriculture, with the tobacco and truck farming industry of the Raleigh economic area being particularly noticeable.

Windsor–Quebec City Major Urban Region

The area between Windsor and Quebec city, consisting of five major metropolises and many other small cities and towns, is the economic heartland of Canada. This area is even more dominant in the Canadian economic system than the Bosnywash urban region in that of the U.S. In 1971, the area that has been defined (Fig. 2.5), on the basis of spheres of influence and population density, as the Windsor-Quebec City axis,[15] contained more than 55% of the population of the country, more than 70% of all the jobs in manufacturing, and the farmers within the area received over 38% of the total farm cash receipts in the nation. Furthermore, Toronto and Montreal, the two major metropolises in the nation, are the location of most of the Canadian headquarters of national and multinational firms operating within the country, the chief stock exchanges, and contain the head offices of the five largest banks (controlling 92% of the bank assets) in the nation. Although there are signs of a small shift in population to the west (particularly Alberta), in 1976 the proportion of the population of Canada residing in the axis had increased to 56%.

Within the context of North America as a whole, however, the recent (1971/76) growth in population has been somewhat less than that experienced in the California urban region and the urban south. This is related to the decline in the birthrate, and the relative decrease in the volume of immigration which accounted for

Fig. 2.5. Location of the CMAs in the Windsor–Quebec City major urban region.

about 23% of the population increase in Canada in the post-war period. Thus, metropolitan growth, which had been quite dramatic in the 1951/1971 period, has now slowed down and has become more manageable.[16] Nevertheless, it is interesting to note that the larger CMAs (those with a population of greater than 0.5 million), except for Montreal, have all experienced quite significant increases in population during the 1971/76 period (Table 2.10), a situation which is in marked contrast to that exhibited by the larger metropolises in the lower Great Lakes urban region to the immediate south and with which this portion of Canada is directly linked.

The continued concentration of population in the axis, and the concomitant growth of the urban areas within the region, are a direct result of a situation in which growth forces in operation throughout the entire country feedback to generate economic expansion within the heartland. This portion of Canada is the location of the production of nearly all the iron and steel, heavy machinery and equipment, motor vehicles, consumer durables, clothing, electronic products, and the by-products of the petrochemical industry that are manufactured within the country. Although information concerning the sources of basic income is not available for economic areas in Canada in the same manner as for the U.S., the distribution of the labor force in selected occupational categories does reveal the importance of manufacturing to most of the metropolises in the axis (Table 2.10). The only two metropolises in which employment in manufacturing appears less important to their economies are Ottawa-Hull (the nation's capital) and Quebec City (the capital city of the Province of Quebec). Governmental employment in Toronto (the capital of the Province of Ontario) is quite large in volume but not dominant compared with the other economic activities of the metropolis.

There are, of course, shifts in the distribution of population taking place within the Windsor-Quebec City urban region, just as there are in the other major urban regions. These shifts are probably crystallized most clearly in the case of Montreal or Toronto, where, over the last few decades, there has been a much faster rate of growth in the metropolitan area of Toronto than Montreal. This has been the result of a steady shift of major headquarter office and banking functions to Toronto, its more diversified manufacturing base, and the dominance of the Toronto Stock Exchange as the capital market for the nation. This relative shift in economic power from Montreal to Toronto has been accelerated slightly by political events, but the shift has not been caused by them for the process has been accumulating over many decades. The greater growth of the Toronto area

Table 2.10. Population of the CMAs in the Windsor-Quebec City urban region, and the distribution of the labor force in these CMAs in three selected categories.

Figure ref.	CMA	Population (in thousands)		Labor force (%)		
		1976	1971	Mfg.	Fin. + Ins.	Govt.
(M)	Montreal	2,759	2,731	28.36	6.31	5.74
(Tor)	Toronto	2,753	2,602	27.47	7.36	5.82
(O-H)	Ottawa-Hull	669	620	8.65	4.69	32.90
(Q)	Quebec	534	501	13.83	4.75	19.35
(H)	Hamilton	525	503	37.48	4.30	4.07
	St. Catharines	298	285	36.35	3.29	4.62
	Kitchener-Waterloo	270	239	41.98	5.12	3.17
	London	264	253	24.43	6.77	6.76
	Windsor	243	249	36.02	4.32	4.44

Source: Population data from 1976 Census of Canada, *Population: Preliminary Counts*, Ottawa: Statistics Canada. Labor force data from Ray, D. M. et al. (1976), *Canadian Urban Trends*, Toronto: Copp-Clark, pp. 88–91.

has also been stimulated by the higher rate of natural increase in the population of the Province of Ontario between 1971 and 1976, a period during which the rate of natural increase in the Province of Quebec was at about the zero population growth level.

Florida Urban Region

The Florida urban region extends almost 400 miles from Jacksonville in the north to Miami in the south. The urban part of the region is now spread almost continuously along the Atlantic shore, completely across the central portion of the state between Daytona Beach and St. Petersburg, and along a considerable portion of the Gulf Coast from north of the Orlando–St. Petersburg metropolitan area to south of Ft. Myers (Fig. 2.6). The pace of urban development in the Florida region has been exceptionally rapid since 1950 (Table 2.1), and the relative rate of increase shows no sign of abatement for it has been the most rapidly growing part of the continent since 1970. One of the interesting features of this growth is that the major metropolises of the area (Table 2.11) have increased in population at a rate similar to that of the urban region as a whole.

The basic reason for this rapid increase in population since World War II is related to the climate of the area, and the advantages that it brings to not just agriculture, but to the recreational and retirement industries. Since 1945, the recreation industry has boomed in North America as a result of (1) almost continuous, until recent years, annual increases in the level of real wages; (2) the increase in length of annual vacations received by most workers in the labor force; and (3) the construction of the interstate highway system which makes it possible for people to travel long distances relatively cheaply in a day or two; (4) the decreasing real price of air fares; and (5) the reduction in family size and increased level of female participation in the labor force which has made it easier for people to take vacations in more "exotic" places.

The impact of retirement has had a significant influence on this population growth, and it will obviously continue to do so in the future as the proportion of older people in population increases. Since 1945, unions have been negotiating more attractive fringe benefit packages involving possibilities for earlier retirement with better post-retirement levels of income and health care benefits. Furthermore, as family size decreases, people are more able to save and consider relocation at an earlier age than they were previously. Added to this is the generally increasing length of life, which makes it possible for people to be reasonably active and independent for more post-retirement years. All these changing health, social, and economic aspects relating to the older population have facilitated the rapid growth of retirement and leisure communities.

These different aspects that have contributed to the growth of the Florida region are represented in the data concerning the economic base of the economic areas of the region (Table 2.12). Though the economic areas, in the case of Florida, tend to be rather large and embrace an area slightly larger than the urban region, they do indicate quite clearly the different nature of this region as compared with the others discussed thus far. First of all, basic earnings received from

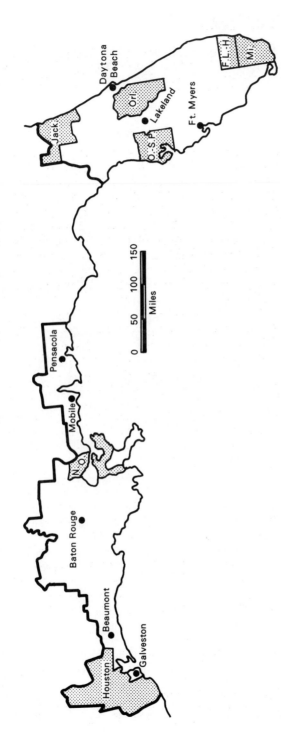

Fig. 2.6. Location of the larger SMSAs in the Florida and Gulf Shore major urban regions.

Table 2.11. Population (in thousands) of the larger SMSAs
in the Florida and Gulf Shore urban regions.

SMSA	1975	1970
Florida urban region		
Miami	1,439	1,268
Tampa–St. Petersburg	1,365	1,088
Ft. Lauderdale–Hollywood	863	620
Jacksonville	701	622
Orlando	585	483
Gulf Shore urban region		
Houston	2,297	1,999
New Orleans	1,094	1,046

manufacturing are, on the whole, relatively low throughout the entire area, although manufacturing is increasing in importance in the region. Compared with the other urban regions, basic earnings from agriculture tend to be quite high, a situation that we would expect from a state well known for its citrus and fresh vegetable industries. Particularly noticeable, however, are the high levels of basic income indicated in the "other" category, which in this case involves transfer (or retirement) incomes and the recreational portion of the service sector. Furthermore, earnings received from employment in federal government activities provide a basic source of income in each economic region, and is particularly important in the case of Jacksonville (defense establishments).

Gulf Shore Urban Region

The fairly continuous strip of urbanization that appears to be developing along the Gulf Shore from Pensacola in the east to the metropolises of Houston–Galveston in the west (Fig. 2.6), has experienced a fairly high rate of growth since 1940 (Table 2.1). The beginning date of high urban growth, therefore, precedes that of the Florida urban region, and during the 1970/75 period it had the second highest growth rate in the nation. Although it is the urban region with the fewest large metropolises (Table 2.11) on the continent, urban development is quite extensive involving not only the large urban areas of Houston and New Orleans, but a number of places in the 200,000–400,000 population range, such as Mobile, Baton Rouge, Beaumont–Port Arthur, and Pensacola. Outside of New Orleans, all of the urban areas within the region have shared in the general growth, with Houston receiving over one-half of the population increase since 1970.

A close analysis of the dominant sources of basic earnings of the more urban economic areas within the region reveals the sources of this post-1940 growth experience, as well as illustrating the diversified economic base of the Gulf Shore complex. Although basic earnings from agriculture are evident in two of the economic areas, this source of basic income appears similar in relative importance

Table 2.12. Economic base of the economic areas in the Florida and Gulf Shore urban regions.

Urban region	1970 Pop.	Agric.	Mining	Mfg.	Fed. + Govt.	Other	Total
Florida							
Miami-Ft. Lauderdale	2,430	4.49	0.24	10.86	2.43	17.98	36.00
Tampa	1,797	4.69	1.28	13.60	2.38	11.91	33.86
Orlando	941	5.29	0.06	19.03	4.24	8.80	37.42
Jacksonville	946	3.72	0.55	12.49	13.46	6.58	36.80
Gulf Shore							
Houston	2,362	1.65	5.87	19.66	0.70	11.59	39.47
New Orleans	2,148	2.29	5.72	16.88	0.70	9.99	35.58
Beaumont	394	0.88	2.58	36.18	0.78	8.81	49.23
Mobile	724	2.34	0.22	23.48	14.95	1.13	42.12
Pensacola	382	1.52	0.15	15.72	33.17		50.56

Source: Berry and Kasarda (1977), pp. 290–293, 296–302.

to the other urban regions except for those in Florida and California. Basic earnings from mining are, however, quite significant in three of the economic areas, and in this respect the Gulf Shore urban region is quite different from those discussed so far. These "mining" basic earnings refer to income received from employment in activities associated with the extraction of oil from land and offshore wells. The demands of World War II stimulated a great expansion of drilling and production in this area that continues unabated.

The development of the petroleum industry provided the stimulus to economic growth in the region, which, prior to 1940, had been stagnant. Capital flooded into the region, and the drilling, production, and refining generated the establishment of plants involved with the manufacture of drilling equipment, heavy machinery, and various products from the petrochemical industry. A further stimulus to the manufacturing base of the western portion of the region came from the establishment of Johnson Space Center ourside Houston in 1963. The location of this facility in the Houston area was the result of a political combination power play involving Rice University, the Exxon Corporation, the city of Houston, the state of Texas, and NASA.[17] Hence the rather large proportion of "other" basic earnings in the Houston and Beaumont economic areas. Thus, as a consequence of the development of the petroleum natural resource base and the heavy investment via NASA, the western portion of the region has a variety of heavy and light industries. In the eastern portion of the region, there has also been fairly large investment from federal sources in defense establishments in Pensacola and Mobile.

Ohio Valley Urban Region

The area that has been defined somewhat narrowly as the Ohio Valley urban region (Fig. 1.9) is the smallest of those included in this discussion. It consists of four large SMSAs (Table 2.13), the land area of which comprises 43% of the total area in the region. The region has been narrowly defined in this manner for a number of reasons. First, the metropolises of Cincinnati, Indianapolis, Columbus, and Dayton appear to be expanding toward each other along the major interstate highway networks that connect them. By the end of this century it is quite possible to envisage direct physical merging of Columbus, Dayton, and Cincinnati, and it is likely that Cincinnati and Dayton will have merged with Indianapolis. This would result in an extensive metropolitan area, containing four major foci, that would be larger than the major metropolitan region of Chicago in the 1970s.

Second, although the sources of earnings of the economic areas (which are slightly larger than the defined Ohio Valley urban region) pertaining to the region (Table 2.13) indicate an economic base quite similar to that of the economic areas of the Lower Great Lakes urban region (see Table 2.5), the population growth of the Ohio Valley region in recent years has been greater. The reasons for this are difficult to determine, for the Ohio Valley cities have been in existence and involved in manufacturing for as long as those in the lower Great Lakes urban region. Perhaps, the greater growth rate is related to the structure of manufacturing in

Table 2.13. Population (in thousands) of the larger SMSAs, and the economic base of the economic areas, in the Ohio Valley urban region.

SMSA and economic area	Cincinnati	Indianapolis	Columbus	Dayton
SMSA population				
1975	1,385	1,147	1,077	837
1970	1,387	1,111	1,017	853
Economic area				
1970 population	1,889	1,613	1,763	1,159
Agriculture	1.83	3.17	1.69	2.25
Mining	0.16	0.32	0.80	0.19
Manufacturing	34.50	33.02	28.91	40.71
Fed. + Govt.	0.54	1.57	3.94	5.94
Other	0.97	1.17	0.50	
Total	38.00	39.25	35.84	49.09

Sources: Berry and Kasarda (1977), pp. 291 and 298, and U.S. Bureau of the Census.

this region, which tends to be quite diversified in the "light" consumer industry direction, as compared with the emphasis on "heavy" industries in the lower Great Lakes.

A third reason for the rather narrow geographic definition of this area is to illustrate the impact of nonmetropolitan growth. Even though the area has been defined so that the four major metropolises comprise a large proportion of the land area, the growth of the metropolitan areas has been quite limited, and a half of the population increase in the region has been experienced in the nonmetropolitan part of the region. The growth of the smaller towns and villages in the nonmetropolitan, rural, part of the region is the result of the decentralization of population, and in a few cases manufacturing plants, to these smaller places. Nonmetropolitan growth of this kind leads to intermetropolitan in-filling and contributes toward the eventual physical merging of the metropolises.

Pacific Northwest and British Columbia

The major urban region of the Pacific northwest and southwestern British Columbia has been amongst those areas that have experienced the greatest rates of increase in population in the last few decades (Table 2.1). While not in the same phenomenal growth category as the Florida urban region, it has, nevertheless, grown since 1960 at a rate remarkably similar to those for the California and Gulf Shore urban regions. Furthermore, the growth in population in the Canadian portion of the area[18] between 1961 and 1976 has been almost the same as that in the U.S. portion of the region between 1960 and 1975. This is in contrast to

Table 2.14. Population (in thousands) of the CMAs and SMSAs, economic base of the economic areas in the U.S. portion, and distribution of the labor force in the CMAs in the Canadian portion, of the Northwest and British Columbia major urban region.

Canadian portion	CMA population		Percent of labor force in CMA				
	1976	1971	Transp.	Extract.	Mfg.	Govt.	Fin. + Ins.
Vancouver	1,136	1,082	10.53	0.79	18.40	5.21	6.58
Victoria	212	196	6.70	0.16	9.82	20.97	5.32

U.S. Portion	SMSA population		Economic areas						
	1975	1970	1970 Pop.	Agric.	Mining	Mfg.	Fed. + Govt.	Other	Total
Seattle–Everett	1,412	1,425 ⎫	2,363	1.25	0.15	27.23	6.12	1.37	36.13
Tacoma	410	408 ⎭							
Portland	1,081	1,007 ⎫	1,637	3.44	0.18	22.48	2.44	3.97	32.50
Salem	207	187 ⎭							
Eugene	241	236	541	2.52	0.75	31.19	3.80	1.42	39.68

Sources: Berry and Kasarda (1977), pp. 243 and 301; U.S. Bureau of the Census, *Estimates of the Population of Counties and Metropolitan Areas, 1975,* Washington, D.C.: U.S. Department of Commerce; 1976 Census of Canada, *Population: Preliminary Counts,* Ottawa: Statistics Canada; and Ray, D. M. et al. (1976), *Canadian Urban Trends,* Toronto: Copp-Clark, pp. 88–91.

the quite different growth rates between the Windsor–Quebec City and lower Great Lakes urban regions in the same period.

There are a number of factors involved in this relatively high rate of growth experienced within the region during the past few decades. First of all, the area is rich in a few natural resources, particularly lumber, fish, and natural gas (British Columbia) from the hinterland. Secondly, the location of the area with respect to Japan and other Far Eastern countries has been a tremendous asset during the post-World War II period. In particular, Vancouver is Canada's chief port for Far Eastern trade, and the leading port for the year-round export of grain.[19] Third, there has been a considerable growth of manufacturing industries in the area (Table 2.14), partly as a result of the raw material base, the expansion of port activities, and the growth of the local consumer market, but primarily because of a unique combination of entrepreneurial drive, technological inventiveness, and marketing which led to the development of the aerospace industry in the Seattle area.[20] By the 1970s, the aerospace industry provided about half of the basic employment in the Puget Sound region. A final factor that should be mentioned is the relatively equable climate of the region, which has led to the establishment of retirement communities in Victoria (which is also the capital of British Columbia) and throughout the Northwest.

The economic base of the region (Table 2.14) is becoming increasingly dominated by manufacturing activities which are less dependent on local resources and local markets, but more dependent on inputs from other regions and exports to other areas for their existence, as time progresses. This area is, therefore, in a sense, one of the last North American urban frontiers, experiencing a shift from dependence on local resources and port activities to an industrial base which is highly interlinked with the rest of the economy of the continent. The location of the area with respect to trans-Pacific trade will continue to be an import asset in the future, and will no doubt result in a continued high level of growth.

DIFFERENCES IN POPULATION GROWTH AMONG THE MAJOR URBAN REGIONS

In the beginning of this chapter there was some brief discussion of Kondratieff cycles, and the major stages of urban development in the U.S. as defined by Borchert, in order to place the 1920/1975 period in perspective. It will be recalled that these dates embrace the early corporate (1890/1940) and advanced corporate (1940/1990?) long cycles, and correspond with the Borchert's 1920/1970 automobile era. The relevance of these long cycles to urban development can be understood with respect to the changing condition of the national economy that occurs, in general, during the 50-year period. Rostow[21] has suggested that Kondratieff cycles can be interpreted with respect to the relative changes in the prices of raw materials with those of finished products. During the first phase of a cycle, the prices of raw materials are increasing relative to those of manufactured products, and this is accompanied by accelerating general inflation, a high range of interest rates, and relative shifts of income to those who are involved in the production of food and energy. Gradually, the relatively high prices of raw materials and food during this phase encourages the development of other or alternate raw material sources, and promotes greater efficiency in use of the materials, so that the price of these basic commodities begins to decrease relative to those of manufactured products.

When this decrease in the relative prices of raw materials and food to those of manufactured goods occurs, the rate of inflation decelerates, and interest rates return to a lower level. This is because manufacturers are receiving more favorable prices for their products and the greater profits are creating a surplus of money capital for investment. Furthermore, the generally lower interest rates, which are in part the result of the great money surplus realized from profits and in part related to the relatively lower and stable prices for raw materials and food, also promotes investment. Thus, during this second phase, there is considerable expansion of the economy, jobs are created, the level of real wages increases, people purchase homes, and the general positive outlook is reflected in an upswing in the birthrate. In the past, the euphoria of an expansionary economy, and relatively low interest rates, has, at the end of the second phase, resulted in overexpansion, wild speculative investments, and a depression in the economy when it becomes apparent that the investments will not yield the expected return.

The general outlines of these phases can be discerned in the actual volume of population increase in North America since 1920 (Table 2.1). From 1920 to 1930 the volume and rate of population increase (16.2%) were quite high, for this is the period that corresponds to the second phase described above. But, over-speculation resulted in the depression of the 1930s, and an era in which population growth was comparatively low (7.6%). World War II stimulated a rather rapid transition through the first phase, the rate of population growth began to increase (1940/50: 15.3%), and it reached a peak during the beginning of the second phase which occurred during the late 1950s and early 1960s (1950/60: 19.5%; 1960/70: 13.8% increase). The economy of North America has, during the latter part of the 1970s, returned to a first-phase set of economic conditions, and a lower rate of population increase.

It must, of course, be recognized that the cyclical changes in the economy, and the rate of population increase, are much affected by the rather rapidly evolving political and social environment. The changing role of women in North American society has had a considerable effect on the birthrate. Also, there have been severe "shocks" to the North American economy from rather high single-stage increases in the price of one basic raw material (petroleum). These forces, which have the effect of prolonging one phase, and shortening the other, may diminish the "amplitude" of the waves, and may even cause a contraction in the length of the cycle. But, the general impact of these economic changes on urbanization, and the relative growth performances of the major urban regions, remain the same.

Shifts in Distribution of Growth

Urban regions are accretions of fixed and immobile capital. The construction of buildings, factories, and urban infrastructure requires accumulations of money sufficient to pay for the labor and materials necessary for the creation of the fixed investments. The financial conditions most conducive to the physical growth of urban areas occur during the second phase in a Kondratieff cycle, when profits are reasonably high, interest rates are low, and employment opportunities are increasing. As it takes some time to assemble land, arrange for investors, design and plan the developments, and build the physical structures, a fairly long period of general conducive economic conditions is necessary for extensive urban investment. Thus, the physical growth of urban areas tends to occur cyclically, with generally high rates of construction during the second phase of a long cycle and lower rates of construction during the first phase.

But, urban growth has to be viewed as taking place on a continent-wide basis, not with respect to just one urban region. The wave-like pattern of population growth that occurs with respect to the continent as a whole does not appear to occur in exactly the same manner with respect to either (1) the major urban regions as a whole or (2) the individual regions themselves. For example, the proportion of the North American population contained within the nine urban regions increased in an upward, wave-like fashion up to 1970/71, but then decreased between 1970/71 and 1975/76 (Table 2.15). Thus, 1970 may be a benchmark period when population growth and economic development began to occur at a greater rate in areas outside the major urban regions of North America.

This decline in the proportion of the population in the 1970s that is contained within the nine major urban regions is related to the fact that between 1930 and 1970 the increase in the proportion of the population contained in the seven regions outside Bosnywash and the lower Great Lakes urban regions offset the decline in the proportion contained in these two (Table 2.15). The growth of Bosnywash and lower Great Lakes urban regions was greater than the continent-wide average up to 1930, but since that time the growth rates of these areas has been less than that of North America as a whole. The 1890/1940, or "early corporate," era, would, therefore, appear to have been a favorable period for urban growth in the Bosnywash and lower Great Lakes urban regions, and the

Table 2.15. Percentage distribution of the North American population among the major urban regions at each time period between 1920 and 1975.

Major urban region	1920/21	1930/31	1940/41	1950/51	1960/61	1970/71	1975/76
Bosnywash	20.32	20.51	20.11	19.73	19.28	19.27	18.83
Lower Great Lakes	17.46	18.21	17.65	17.39	17.19	16.57	15.94
California	3.33	3.92	4.44	5.95	7.40	8.28	8.35
The urban south	5.60	5.53	5.65	5.65	5.36	5.33	5.38
Windsor–Quebec City	4.02	4.07	4.17	4.40	4.92	5.30	5.29
Florida	0.56	0.83	1.03	1.37	2.13	2.67	3.16
The Gulf Shore	1.72	1.85	1.95	2.33	2.63	2.78	2.88
Ohio Valley	2.66	2.56	2.53	2.58	2.68	2.67	2.61
The Northwest and B.C.	1.56	1.65	1.77	2.13	2.22	2.40	2.43
Total	57.23	59.13	59.30	61.53	63.81	65.27	64.87

1940/1990(?), or "advanced corporate" era, much less favorable. Furthermore, the relative decline of the lower Great Lakes urban region appears to have been much greater than that of the Bosnywash area. The questions that need answering with respect to these two areas, therefore, concern the reasons for the change in growth rate from being above the continent average prior to 1930 to below the continent average after 1940, and the greater decline in growth of the lower Great Lakes area vis-à-vis Bosnywash.

The answers with respect to the growth performances of Bosnywash and the lower Great Lakes area will, of course, illuminate the different patterns of change that have occurred in the other seven urban regions, and the rest of the continent, for all of the sections are interlinked. The Ohio Valley urban region, which coexists with the lower Great Lakes urban region, has been maintaining a growth rate at about the continent average since 1920, although the 1970/75 evidence may indicate some relative decline in the future. Equally as interesting, the Windsor-Quebec City urban region, which is also tied closely to the lower Great Lakes urban region, experienced a growth rate between 1940 and 1970 that was well above the continent average, but between 1970 and 1975 at about the average. The reasons for these differences and recent changes need to be unraveled.

Four regions (California, Florida, the Gulf Shore, and Northwest and British Columbia) have grown at rates above the continent average since 1920. As a consequence, they have increased the share of the North American population found within their respective regions since that date, though the increases in each case seem to have been greater since 1940. The pattern of growth in these four areas would, therefore, appear to offset those of Bosnywash and the lower Great Lakes, and may well be related to economic forces operating in the 1940/1990, or "advanced corporate," era. Also of interest is the greater slowing down in the rate of increase in the proportion of the North American population located in the California and Northwest and British Columbia urban regions between 1970/71 and 1975/76.

The last regional shift that requires some explanation concerns the fluctuating proportion of the North American population found in the region of the "urban south." In this case there is no distinct pattern of change since 1940, for the percentage figures fluctuate throughout the entire 55-year time period. Recent trends (1970/75) would suggest that the proportion of the North American population contained within this region would continue to increase, for there has been a considerable increase in the population of the larger metropolitan areas in the last census period. The explanation may well lie in a mixture of economic and social factors, some of which are unique to this area. It is, therefore, necessary to examine some of the theories that have been developed to account for regional differences in growth performances and changes within individual regions.

NOTES

[1] D. Harvey, "The Geography of Accumulation," *Antipode*, Vol. 7, No. 2 (1975), pp. 9–21.
[2] N. D. Kondratieff, "The Long Wave in Economic Life," *Review of Economics and Statistics*, No. 17 (1935), pp. 105–155.

[3] R. A. Walker, "The Transformation of Urban Structure in the Nineteenth Century and the Beginnings of Suburbanization" in K. Cox (ed.), *Urbanization and Conflict in Market Societies* (Chicago: Maaroufa Press, 1977), pp. 165-212.

[4] R. A. Walker, "A Theory of Suburbanization: Capitalism and the Construction of Urban Space in the United States" in M. Dear and A. Scott (eds.), *Urbanization and Urban Planning* (Chicago: Maaroufa Press, 1979).

[5] J. R. Borchert, "America's Changing Metropolitan Regions," *Annals of the Association of American Geographers*, Vol. 62, No. 2 (1972), pp. 352-373.

[6] L. A. Swatridge, *The Bosnywash Megalopolis: A Region of Great Cities* (New York: McGraw-Hill, 1971).

[7] C. E. Browning (ed.), *Population and Urbanized Area Growth in Megalopolis* (Chapel Hill: University of North Carolina, Department of Geography, 1974).

[8] M. Yeates and B. Garner, *The North American City*, 3rd ed. (New York: Harper & Row, 1980), Ch. 4.

[9] R. C. Otte, *Farming in the City's Shadow, Urbanization of Land and Changes in Farm Output in Standard Metropolitan Statistical Areas, 1960-70* (Washington, D.C.: U.S. Department of Agriculture, ERS Report No. 250, 1974).

[10] A. B. Leman and I. A. Leman, *Great Lakes Megalopolis: From Civilization to Ecumenization* (Ottawa: Supply and Services, 1976).

[11] A. R. Pred, *Major Job-Providing Organizations and Systems of Cities* (Washington, D.C.: Association of American Geographers, Resource Paper No. 27, 1974).

[12] D. W. Lantis, R. Steiner and A. E. Karinen, *California: Land of Contrasts* (Dubuque, Iowa: Kendall Hunt, 1977).

[13] B. J. L. Berry and D. C. Dahmann, "Population Redistribution in the United States in the 1970s," *Population and Development Review*, Vol. 3, No. 4 (1977), pp. 443-471.

[14] L. F. Wheat, *Urban Growth in the Non-Metropolitan South* (Farnborough, Hants.: Lexington Books, 1976).

[15] M. Yeates, *Main Street: Windsor to Quebec City* (Toronto: Macmillan of Canada, 1975).

[16] L. S. Bourne, "Some Myths of Canadian Urbanization: Reflections on the 1976 Census and Beyond," *Urbanism Past and Present*, No. 5 (1977-78), pp. 1-11.

[17] M. E. Palmer and M. N. Rush, "Houston" in J. Adams (ed.), *Contemporary Metropolitan America: Twentieth Century Cities* (Cambridge, Mass.: Ballinger, 1976) pp. 107-149.

[18] E. M. Gibson, "The Urbanization of the Strait of Georgia Region" (Ottawa: Environment Canada, Geography Paper No. 57, 1976).

[19] W. G. Hardwick, *Vancouver* (Don Mills: Collier-Macmillan, 1974).

[20] R. A. Erickson, "The Regional Impact of Growth Firms: The Case of Boeing, 1963-68," *Land Economics*, No. 50 (1974), pp. 127-136.

[21] W. W. Rostow, "Regional Change in the Fifth Kondratieff Upswing" in D. C. Perry and A. J. Watkins (eds.), *The Rise of the Sunbelt Cities* (Beverly Hills, Calif.: Sage Publications, Urban Affairs Annual Reviews, Vol. 14, 1977).

Chapter 3

Causes of the differential growth patterns

A number of different explanations can be presented concerning the reasons for the variations in growth among the major urban regions of North America. These different explanations relate to the influences on the economic base of the major regions, for the raison d'étre of any city, metropolis, or urban region is economic as expressed by the volume of income generated through employment and financial transfers. Although the focus on explanations for the location of economic activity may appear to imply consideration of only economic factors, this is not the case. There are many political, social, and personal preference influences on the location of economic activity. Furthermore, the way in which the explanations are presented and interpreted depends on the individual's interpretation of the manner in which the economic and political system operates. There is, in effect, no "explanation" in the social sciences that is not ideologically based in one way or another. It is hoped that this observation becomes clearer as the chapter progresses.

The various hypotheses that have been offered as explanations of differential growth among the major urban regions can be grouped into four categories:[1] (1) economic convergence, (2) the staples approach, (3) economic divergence, (4) economic control. Some of these are quite closely related, such as the staples and circular and cumulative causation approaches, but they differ in complexity and the extent to which they permit the inclusion of various interrelationships within the economy, and between economic systems and social or political systems. In general, the various explanations increase in complexity from (1) to (4), and, as with most complex arguments, the presentation of the more complex explanations may be oversimplified. Nevertheless, the range of perspectives on the issue of differential growth cannot be ignored.

55

ECONOMIC CONVERGENCE

The economic convergence model suggests that there is a tendency for economic growth rates to converge over a long period of time.[2] Proponents of this perspective point to evidence which indicates that the early growth of the metropolises and cities in the Bosnywash and lower Great Lakes urban regions has been offset in recent decades by the more rapid growth of urban areas in the west and south. The economic convergence model suggests that the growth rates in the areas that are now growing more rapidly will eventually decrease, such as appears to be happening in the case of the California urban region, and the previously slower growing areas will experience a resurgence. There is, therefore, a general view that regional growth rates will, in the long run, converge on some equilibrium, with a continuous fluctuation of the different areas over a long period of time around the average continent-wide rate of growth. The mechanisms leading to this continuous readjustment to an equilibrium are considered to be regional differences in factors associated with income and rates of return on fixed capital investments. It will become apparent, as these two broad categories are described, that many of the factors are interlinked and that all, in general, refer to differences in the rates of return to investments of any kind.

The tendency to convergence during the time period under discussion can be seen most clearly in the changing distribution of per capita incomes as a percent of the U.S. total in Table 3.1. Though the regions in this table are based on aggregations of states, and do not correspond directly to the major urban regions being analyzed, there is a rough comparison that is sufficient to demonstrate convergence and raise questions about the factors leading to this convergence. The most noticeable features in Table 3.1 are, perhaps, the wide divergence of per capita incomes in 1920 and the limited divergence of per capita incomes in

Table 3.1. Regional distribution of per capita incomes as a percent of the U.S., 1920/1975.

Region	1975	1970	1960	1950	1940	1930	1920
U.S.	100	100	100	100	100	100	100
New England	108	108	109	106	121	129	124
Middle Atlantic	108	113	116	116	124	140	134
East North Central	104	105	107	112	112	111	108
West North Central	98	95	93	94	84	82	87
South Atlantic	90	86	77	74	69	56	59
East South Central	79	74	67	63	55	48	52
West South Central	91	85	83	81	70	61	72
Mountain	92	90	95	96	92	83	100
Pacific	111	110	118	121	138	130	135

Sources: *Historical Statistics of the United States, Colonial Times to 1970*, Washington, D.C.: Department of Commerce, 1975, p. 242; *Survey of Current Business, 56*, August, 1976, p. 17.

1975. In fact, if the per capita income figures were to be modified according to the relative costs of living in the different parts of the country, the divergence between the north and the south would be even less, and the people living in the Pacific states would probably appear to have even higher levels of real per capita income.

Of particular interest, with respect to the changing distribution of population among the major urban regions in the previous chapter, are the rather rapid changes in divergence that appear to have commenced around 1940. This is especially noticeable in the case of the groups of states that form the "south" (the South Atlantic, East South Central, and West South Central) and include the "urban south," the Gulf Shore, and the Florida urban regions. There has been a rapid rise in level of per capita income in the 35-year period from 50-60% of the U.S. average to 80-90% of the national level. On the other hand, the general level of per capita incomes of these groups of states (New England, Middle Atlantic, and East North Central) that embrace the Bosnywash and lower Great Lakes urban regions have decreased from 110-140% of the U.S. average to 104-108% of the national level. A similar convergence is also observable, commencing at about 1940, for the Pacific states, which include the California and Northwest urban regions.

These regional differences in per capita income levels reflect variations in wage rates in the various parts of the nation. The questions that arise, therefore, relate to the factors influencing differences in wage rates over the past six decades in the different parts of the continent. If this question is approached with respect to the recipients of the wages, labor, then the matter can be examined with respect to labor productivity and the degree to which labor is organized to bargain for its share of the fruits of production. The productivity of labor is, in general, related to its own quality and the quality of the productive capital with which it is working. The quality of labor is in part related to its level of education and training for work in fairly regimented situations. There may be some substance, therefore, to an argument that the south tended to suffer from a fairly backward system of education, and that the improved level of income in this area is partly related to a decrease in differences in level of education between that section of the U.S. and the rest of the nation in recent years.

But, probably the most important influence on labor productivity is the efficiency of the productive capital with which it is working. The metropolises in the older parts of the continent tend to have high levels of fixed capital investment in buildings and factories which are less efficient (from the point of view of production) than the latest technologies. By comparison, metropolis and cities located in parts of the country that have only recently experienced heavy industrialization tend to have much newer plants which can take advantage of the most efficient technologies in production. Thus, convergence of growth rates tends to result from the different phases of capital investment, and while the faster growing areas today may receive the benefits from their relatively newer plants and greater levels of efficiency, in time these plants will also age and the regions will begin to decrease in rate of growth.

To the regional differences in level of per capita investment in new technologies must also be added regional variations in industry-mix. Industry-mix refers to the proportion of the manufacturing base of a region that consists of high-growth and low-growth industries in a national (and international) context. Some types of manufacturing are growing rapidly because they are producing goods that are in great demand (such as electronics industries) while others are not growing, or even in decline, because the demand for their output is stagnant or decreasing. A metropolis, and region, which is said to have a "good" industry-mix is, therefore, one which has a large proportion of its employment involved with high-growth industries, whereas those with a "poor" industry-mix have a large proportion of their employment in low-growth industries. Much of the relative decline of Bosnywash, and particularly the lower Great Lakes, urban region is attributable to a poor industry-mix. The concentration of older, heavy industries in the lower Great Lakes region has been commented upon in Chapter 2.

But, wage rates, the general level of incomes, and the rate of economic growth in a region, are not only related to the productivity of labor, but also the degree to which labor is organized to bargain for the fruits of its production. In a classic study of changes in the location of manufacturing in the U.S. between 1930 and 1960, which quite nicely involves the transitional period around the 1940s, Fuchs[3] noted that the greater comparative growth of manufacturing employment in the south was related to lower levels of unionization in the region. The general absence of unionization permitted the payment of wages below those negotiated by the unions in the north, and manufacturing plants appeared to have relocated accordingly. The general increase in comparative levels of income in the south since 1940 could, therefore, be attributable to the way in which labor has become organized in the region since that time, and is now receiving wages at nationally negotiated rates. The impact of the higher wage rates for union labor in the south has, naturally, had a positive effect on the earnings of nonunion labor. Thus, over time, economic convergence occurs as a result of the national, and continental, organization of labor, as well as the eventual convergence of the efficiency of fixed capital investments and the industry-mix.

The general movement of population, which is related to employment opportunities, will, therefore, tend to even out regional inequalities. The responses can be examined with respect to income differences and employment differences. If the general levels of income are higher in one region than another, as in the case of the Pacific region vis-à-vis the rest of the U.S., perhaps as a result of the labor scarcities, then people will move to take advantage of the greater economic opportunities. In time, the labor shortages may disappear (as they are now doing in the Pacific area) and the rate of population growth will fall and converge on the national average. The reduction in labor scarcity will cause wage rates to hold level, and per capita incomes to converge on to the national average. Thus, the response of labor to interregional differences in income levels through interregional migration is one basic mechanism that, in the long run, will even out inequalities in population growth and economic welfare between regions.

If wage rates, and per capita income levels, are much lower in one or more regions than they are elsewhere, then manufacturers and the owners of other enterprises might move there to take advantage of the lower labor costs. The movement is, of course, predicated upon the locational aspects being suitable and the quality of the labor not being so inefficient as to offset the wage rate differential. With the generation of new employment opportunities, rural dwellers within the region will seek employment in the new plants and enterprises, for the wage rates in these newer activities will invariably be higher than those received from employment related to agriculture. It is interesting in this regard to note the observation of Lonsdale and Browning[4] that industrial activities which have plants located in the metropolitan areas in the north (and elsewhere) usually have plants located in the smaller towns and rural areas of the south.

This then brings us to an interpretation of what may be happening in the "urban south." The situation in the urban south, it will be recalled, is that although it has experienced a steady increase in population since 1920, it has not grown at a rate faster than that for the nation as a whole. The relatively high rate of natural increase in the region has, in effect, been offset until 1970 by a general out-migration of the younger black population. The area has, however, increased in average level of per capita income as compared with the rest of the U.S. This increase in level of per capita income has been associated with (1) the movement of manufacturing to the large and small urban places in the region and (2) the location of a large number of defense establishments in the region. The convergence hypothesis leads us to interpret the growth of manufacturing in the area to be the result of the attraction of lower labor costs. The employment for the new industrial jobs has come from the rural parts of the local region, and there has been little in-migration from elsewhere in the nation (until recently) to take advantage of the new jobs because of the generally lower levels of income received by workers in the region.

It may be predicted that this situation is now changing, as is indicated by the higher rate of population increase experienced within the region since 1970. As per capita income levels in the region converge on the national, the area becomes more attractive to potential in-migrants because of the jobs, small town atmosphere, and more attractive climate. Furthermore, the transition from a rural to an urban economy has brought with it an improvement in some of the basic services, such as education and health care facilities, in which the region had previously been deficient. During the next decade the "urban south" may, therefore, continue to experience a relative increase in per capita income levels, and also experience population growth above the continental average as a result of in-migration.

The emphasis on defense establishments as important components of the economic areas within the region can also be explained within the premises of the convergence hypothesis. If the convergence hypothesis is accepted as a tenable explanation of what happens when there are regional differences in per capita income and rates of economic growth, the public policy implications are to interfere as little as possible in the natural course of events. There is a tendency toward an equilibrium as a result of the play of natural market forces, so the state should interfere as little as possible in the location of private business activities. Critical conditions of deprivation can be met by the reallocation of resources through unemployment benefits, social security, and welfare payments. If the stagnation in the economy occurs for a lengthy period of time, then some increase in activity can be generated by the transfer of some "industries" over which the state does have control, such as defense establishments. It is quite evident that in the urban south basic income realized as a result of transfer payments through the location of defense facilities in the region has become an important support for the region.

The question then arises concerning when basic support of this kind should be withdrawn. It is now becoming quite evident that parts of Bosnywash, and a large portion of the lower Great Lakes urban regions, are converging on the U.S. average with respect to per capita income and are lagging behind the rest of the continent in terms of population and economic growth. In fact, if costs of living are taken into account, these two urban regions are probably at below the continent average. The use of federal transfers may well be exacerbating this condition. For example, Peterson and Muller[5] contend that "On a per capita basis, the Pacific states receive more than twice as much federal revenue as the Great Lakes states and 80% more than the Mid-Atlantic states." In a particular case, in 1976 expenditures by the federal government in the state of New York totalled $26.3 billion, but monies received by the federal government from personal and corporate tax payments totalled $33.7 billion.[6]

The net impact of government transfers of this type has been a fueling of the economies of the sections of the west and south, and a dampening down of economic growth in the lower Great Lakes and Bosnywash urban regions. Thus, given the situation that now exists where the poor industry-mix and generally older fixed capital investments of these regions are leading to unfavorable rates of growth, it is probably time to reconsider some of the patterns of defense and purchasing outlays that have been developed by the federal government over the past 30 to 40 years. Although the geographic direction of expenditure patterns cannot be changed quickly, the fact that federal disbursements (defense and general expenditures) have been used to foster convergence does mean that similar policies can also be used to help regenerate the economies of areas where the dampening of economic growth may have become excessive.

THE STAPLES APPROACH

Regional differences in economic growth are also often related to an uneven distribution, availability, and marketability of natural resources. This particular view as used extensively by the Canadian economic historian Harold Innes in his interpretation of the varying patterns of economic growth in Canada. He was particularly concerned with the way in which the different regions depended on the production of specific commodities that appeared to be staple to their economies, and examining the way in which external demand for these "staples" influenced the growth of the area. In the context of the major urban regions of North America, it has been observed that the economic growth of a number of areas was stimulated by the production of certain commodities, and that perhaps stagnation in a few areas is also associated with a decline in demand for particular raw materials. Thus, the growth and stagnation of some areas may be interpreted in the context of the staples hypothesis.

Probably the best example that has been presented of a region in which economic growth has been stimulated by the development of a particular resource base is in the Gulf Shore urban region. In this region, two economic areas (Houston and New Orleans) have a significant proportion (nearly 6%) of their basic earnings received from income generated from mining associated with the extraction of petroleum. The extraction of petroleum from this area became economically feasible due to the great demand for domestic supplies during World War II, and the use of petroleum as a base for the production of numerous synthetics, such as plastics and artificial rubber. Thus, petroleum can be regarded as a staple to the development of the region, but it must be noted that it did not lead to a high rate of economic growth until there was sufficient external demand both for the raw material and the by-products. In a similar fashion, the strong external demand for (1) agricultural products grown (and often packaged) within the Stockton and Sacramento economic areas, (2) lumber and wood pulp produced within the Vancouver and Pacific northwest economic areas, and (3) tobacco grown in the economic area surrounding Raleigh, may also be regarded as factors leading to urban growth in these areas.

On the other side of the coin, a decline in the demand for a product that is staple to an area may lead to stagnation. For example, the recent decline in population within the Pittsburgh SMSA has been noted, and part of this decline may be attributed to the changing demand for a raw material that has been a staple product of the region. In the economic area pertaining to Pittsburgh, nearly 3% of the basic earnings in the region are derived from employment in the mining of coal. The production of coal in the area led to the establishment of the iron and steel smelting industry, and the coal itself was also in great demand as a source of energy for steam engines and heating. With the increasing use of oil-burning power generators during the 1950s and 1960s, and the replacement of coal-fired smelters by electrical smelters during the 1960s and 1970s, the demand for coal decreased. This has led to economic stagnation in many of the mining and industrial towns within the Pittsburgh economic area. Rising prices for oil, and scarcities, during the middle and late 1970s may, however, lead to a resurgence in the importance of this staple product to the economic area in the near future.

The Staples Approach and the Economic Base Concept

The staples concept, with its emphasis on the identification of economic resources produced within a region that generate income as a result of external demand, is associated directly with the economic base concept. The economic base approach focusses attention on activities that are considered basic to a region, and attributes changes in economic growth to changes in the external demand for these basic activities. The staples approach directs attention, in exactly the same way, toward changes in the external demand for raw materials and agricultural products produced within a region. The concepts are, therefore, quite similar, with the staples approach being more narrowly focussed on the activity generated from natural resources and those industries directly related to the resource base.

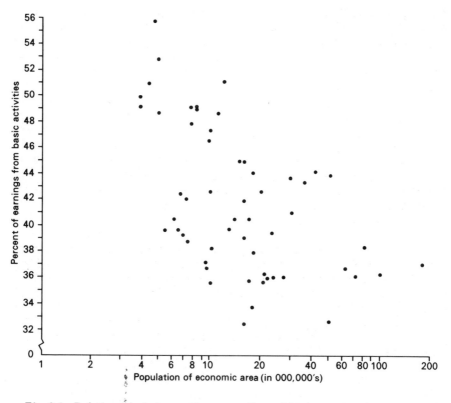

Fig. 3.1. Relationship between the proportion of basic earnings in an economic area and population size.

The more general economic base approach, therefore, states that:

Total income with an urban region	=	Total income derived from basic activities	+	Total income derived from non-basic activities

The basic activities are those that involve the production of goods sold beyond the urban region. The nonbasic activities are those concerned with the production of goods and services that are consumed by the inhabitants of the urban region. In practical terms, it is usually quite difficult to determine precisely what are basic and nonbasic activities, for some are involved in the production of goods and services that are both exported and consumed locally. Furthermore, it is usually difficult to obtain income data, and often employment is used as a surrogate. As a consequence, estimation procedures are commonly used to derive the different components of the basic/nonbasic equation.

Estimation procedures have, in fact, been used for the calculation of the economic base information, pertaining to economic areas, in Chapter 2. The "Total" column in each economic base table indicates the proportion of the earnings in each economic area that are estimated to be "basic" to that region. Thus, in the case of Syracuse, the "total" proportion of earnings considered to be basic to the economic area is (from Table 2.5) 40.63%. The proportion of earnings within the economic area that are nonbasic is, therefore, 59.37%. In general, the proportion of earnings that is considered basic within an economic area decreases as the population size of the area increases (Fig. 3.1). This is because the larger economic areas contain a much more diverse set of manufacturing and service activities and are more able to provide from local sources the vast variety of different demands of the local population. The negative relationship between the proportion of earnings from basic activities and population size does, however, exhibit numerous "deviant" cases. For example, the Richmond economic area (population 1 million) has a smaller proportion of its total earnings derived from basic activities than the New York conglomeration (population 18 million). Deviations such as these make use of the economic base model for predictive purposes impossible,[7] but the general concept is useful as an approach to analyzing the important elements in the economic structure of a region. The model assumes that the economic health of an area can be examined most effectively by focussing on the basic activities, for it is the performance of this component which determines whether the area will grow, stagnate, or decline.

ECONOMIC DIVERGENCE

The economic divergence approach has been articulated most clearly in the circular and cumulative causation model. As applied to the growth of large urban regions, the model indicates how, once something triggers growth in an area, powerful forces come into play which stimulate additional growth by attracting other economic activities or by the expansion of existing ones. As a result, growth is cumulative and may well continue for a long period of time. Thus, a particular region may build continuously upon this initial advantage and increase in wealth at a rate much faster than those that did not experience a similar stimulus of economic activity. Rather than convergence, there may well, therefore, be a divergence of growth rates, with some regions appearing to have an advantageous position for many decades.

When this approach is applied to trends in growth in the major urban regions of North America, it is quite apparent that divergence existed for quite a long period of time up to about 1950. This divergence occurred particularly with respect to the Bosnywash and lower Great Lakes urban regions, and appears to have existed continuously since 1920 in the case of the west coast regions. The convergence that appears to have been occurring since 1940/50 may not, therefore, be a convergence at all, but may be an early stage of divergence. The southern, like the western urban regions, will continue to grow faster than the others, and the older urban regions will continue to grow slowly or stagnate. The important questions that need to be answered in the context of the divergence approach are, therefore, (1) What causes the initial growth stimulus?; (2) Why is growth cumulative?; (3) Why does growth continue over a long period of time?; (4) Are there any processes that may cause growth to cease?; and (5) Can the cumulative growth process be reversed and cumulative decline occur? The first three of these questions are answered directly by the processes incorporated within the structure of the circular and cumulative causation model.

The Circular and Cumulative Causation Model

The model, which is outlined in Figure 3.2, is articulated with respect to changes occurring as a result of an implantation of manufacturing. This is because the Bosnywash and lower Great Lakes urban regions grew fastest during the period of rapid growth in manufacturing in the 1890/1940 early corporate era. This was the age in which the large family industrial empires (such as those of Carnegie, Rockefeller, and Durant) transformed themselves into national corporations (U.S. Steel, Standard Oil, and General Motors). The location of most of the manufacturing establishments was, therefore, the result of decisions by individual entrepreneurs. These locational decisions were frequently made in the context

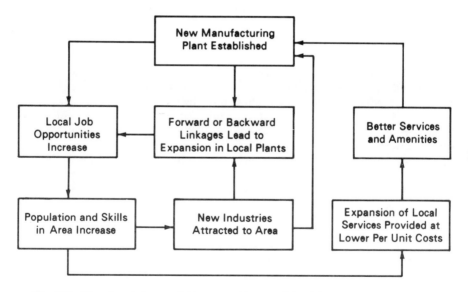

Fig. 3.2. Circular and cumulative causation model with respect to the implantation of a new manufacturing firm in an urban area.

of the home location of the family and the economic advantages that led to the initial establishment of the family business.[8] Though the economic advantages, such as local raw materials, may have become depleted within a few decades, industrial activity still continued because of the developed fixed capital investments and the trained local labor force.

The circular and cumulative causation model begins, then, with the establishment of a new manufacturing concern (Fig. 3.2) as a result of some local entrepreneurial initiative. The impact of this new plant on the local economy is then multiplied by two interrelated processes. The first relates to the *direct* increase in local job opportunities, which leads to some population increase and the creation of a wider variety of skills in the local labor force. This direct impact on the local population and local labor force provides a greater attraction for other industries to enter the area, and also creates an additional demand for more local services (such as schools, sewerage, water, etc.) which, because of the population increase, can now be provided at lower per unit costs. This latter affect on services leads to a better level of local service provision which might well prove attractive to other plants that might be considering locating in the area.

The second interrelated process concerns the *indirect* impact on industrial activity and population growth due to the forward and backward linkages that may well be created by the input and output requirements of the newly established plant. Forward linkages are created locally if the output of the new plant serves, in some way, to expand marginally the operation of a local concern. This expansion may occur by the new plant marketing its output through a local wholesaler, using the facilities of local transport company to ship the goods to their market, requiring packaging which can be supplied by a local firm, etc. Backward linkages are created when the new firm purchases from local sources some necessary inputs to its manufacturing process. The result of these forward and backward linkages is also an increase in local job opportunities, which act as a stimulus to local population growth, and the provision of local services.

The two processes are, therefore, circular and cumulative to the extent that they interact with one another. The result is that the direct impact of the new plant is multiplied due to the indirect impact on local industries via forward and backward linkages, and the increased set of skills in the workforce and enhanced quality and range of local services. It is, however, apparent that the magnitude of these indirect effects will not be the same for each urban area. In some urban areas the possibilities of local forward and backward linkages might be quite limited and may never materialize. In these situations the new firm will have to develop forward and backward linkages with plants outside the region, and the impact on the local economy will be minimal. Thus, the multiplier effect, that is, the direct plus indirect local impacts of the new plant, will be quite small. In general, the larger an urban area, the greater the range of activities in the local area and the greater the possibility for local linkages. The multiplier effect of a new plant on a large integrated urban region should, therefore, be much larger than in small urban areas, and continue over a fairly long period of time due to the steady accretion of fixed capital which takes a number of years to depreciate.

Agglomeration Economies and Scale Diseconomies. The basic problem, however, with the circular and cumulative causation approach is that it is apparent the population and economic base of some urban regions do not increase indefinitely. The reasons for this are many, varying from a poor industrial-mix, a decline in demand for the output of the firms in the area, decreasing productivity of the existing fixed capital investments, to depletion of the local natural resource base. These aspects of economic stagnation have been discussed in the previous two sections. An additional set of factors that needs to be considered concern the size of the urban region itself and the way that these relate to the opposing economic forces of agglomeration, on the one hand, and diseconomies of scale, on the other.

Agglomeration Economies. Generally, the concentration of manufacturing activities in urban regions provides firms with a range of benefits that they would not realize in smaller towns or cities. These benefits are, therefore, external to the financial operation of the firm and are referred collectively as external economies arising from the agglomeration of other plants and firms in the local area, as well as the advantages of the urban area itself. Although it is difficult to define the exact nature of these economies, it is possible to discuss them in the context of those relating to the urban region and those concerning the industrial structure of the area.

Urbanization economies are realized from the existing physical structure and range of services within the urban region. Although there are many different types of urbanization economies, the most obvious are derived from the local infrastructure, which includes the real capital invested in utilities, roads, transportation, commercial facilities, educational and research establishments, etc. As a consequence, plants do not have to create these resources or provide these facilities themselves, and the range of these facilities tends to increase with size of urban region. An important component of the local service infrastructure is the availability of short-term credit, which is often needed to provide working capital to even out the periodic fluctuations in income as against the weekly or monthly requirements for disbursements of wages and salaries. In large urban areas, there are a number of banks who are in a position to make decisions concerning loans of these kinds, and the firm can "shop around" for the most favorable interest rates.

Localization economies are realized from the relationship between the firm and other plants in the area, and the range of skills that these different plants have helped to develop in the local labor force. In such situations a plant might be able to develop a variety of forward and backward linkages, which makes it possible to subcontract sections of orders and even accept larger contracts than it can fulfill by itself because of the availability of other local plants with surplus capacity. The existence of other manufacturing concerns also results in a large local labor force, and for new manufacturing plants this means that the costs of training do not have to be absorbed by itself, but, in effect have been absorbed by all the other firms in the region. The support services of other firms is also vital with respect to the maintenance of machinery, repairs, and for the manufacture of parts. One of the great disadvantages of isolated locations is the time-delay involved in obtaining spare parts.

Diseconomies of Scale. Although these urbanization and localization economies, which are so important to the operation of the circular and cumulative causation model, may imply a continuous increase in economies with size of urban region, it is also evident that certain diseconomies can develop as well. For example, competition between firms may force up the costs of land, factory space, and local wage rates. When a new firm enters, with brand new capital equipment, it may be able to take advantage of the more productive capital and pay higher wage rates to lure skilled workers from other local industries. This may well cause the older plants to discontinue operations, for they will be unable to compete for labor. In these situations, a general decline in manufacturing within the region may occur as the complex fabric of interlinkages falls apart, and the localization economies disintegrate.

Urbanization diseconomies also occur when transportation becomes overloaded and rail or road facilities become so congested that it is difficult to transport goods not only within the urban region but to and from the urban area. Probably a most pervasive form of urban diseconomy results from the environmental and neighborhood pollution created by many heavy manufacturing plants. Parts of an urban region may become most unattractive both visually, and from the point of view of the health of the residents, and the portion of the population that can afford to move away does so. This leads to a decline in the population of the area, a decrease in the range of local stills, and possibly even abandonment of the local housing stock. Forces of disagglomeration of this kind have generally been associated with parts of urban areas, such as central cities, but such features may now be beginning to operate with respect to large macro-urban regions as well.

Why Urban Regions May Cease To Grow. The interplay between the economic forces of agglomeration and diseconomies of scale provides one avenue for explaining why population growth in an urban region may cease, and even be reversed. As metropolitan areas grow, the forces of urban agglomeration yield greater productive efficiencies, and output per capita rises. There comes a time, however, when the diseconomies of scale offset the economies of urban agglomeration, and output per capita levels may begin to decrease. In these situations, new plants look elsewhere for locations and some of the labor force begins to seek jobs in other urban regions as well. The problem, however, is (as has been discussed in Chapter 1) that it is difficult to determine the size range of metropolitan areas in which these diseconomies begin to be pervasive.

It is, in fact, quite probable that the size at which the urban region ceases to grow is more related to noneconomic than economic factors. Certainly, in the case of large sections of the lower Great Lakes and Bosnywash urban regions, the forces of disagglomeration appear to have become more influential than the advantages of urban agglomeration. But, other factors have also influenced the out-migration of the population and economic activities from these areas. Important among these are: the year-round opportunities for leisure and recreation in warmer climates; the diminution of the importance of extended family ties as families become smaller and divorce more common; greater levels of inter-regional accessibility arising from highway and air transport improvements, which make it possible for people and industries to locate anywhere in the continent but still have rapid physical access to places many thousands of miles away when necessary; and the ease of communications.

The Impact of Decline

In Figure 3.3 the affect of a contraction in manufacturing is expressed in the format of the circular and cumulative causation model. The contraction of manufacturing in the urban region has both direct and indirect impacts. The direct impact can be traced through the reduction in local job opportunities that result and the negative affect that this has on the size of the local population. With respect to service infrastructure, the decline in tax revenue received from the manufacturing plant, and the reduction in size of the taxpaying population base, mean that economies of scale cannot be realized in the local service infrastructure, which implies the provision of services at higher per capita costs. This leads to a reduction in the level of local services which can lead to further declines in the manufacturing base due to a loss of significant urbanization economies.

Following the indirect impact, the loss of a manufacturing plant means a reduction in the volume of forward and backward inter-industry linkages, which leads to a disintegration of localization economies. As a consequence, local job opportunities decrease, with associated negative impacts on the population of the area and local services. The decrease in local services, which occurs as a result

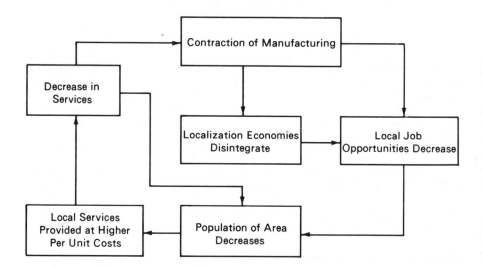

Fig. 3.3. Effect of a contraction in manufacturing employment expressed in the format of the circular and cumulative causation model.

of both the direct and indirect impacts, also leads to an out-migration of some of the local population due to a deterioration in the quality of such services as schooling, public transport, and local support agencies. Thus, there is a multiplier effect of a decline in the local industrial base that is similar to that realized when industrial activity expands.

The negative multiplier effect does not, however, tend to be as large as might be implied from the model, particularly in relatively large metropolises. In a study of 30 SMSAs, Rust[9] concludes that "under continued economic nongrowth, metropolitan areas become extremely resistant to decline in population size." This is because only a small portion of the population of a metropolitan area is, in fact, highly mobile, the vast majority being extremely cautious about moving. The age group that has the greatest mobility consists of those between the ages of 15 and 25 years. People in this age group tend to be unmarried and have few or no dependents, they do not own property, they are more likely to adapt to new places, and they are more flexible in the types of employment they are willing to accept as well as being more trainable. Once a proportion of this portion of the population has left, there are few others who are highly mobile. The remianing majority is prepared to accept lower paying jobs or part-time work, commute outside the area, or withdraw from the labor force, rather than leave the community. This leads to a general decline in per capita incomes, which exacerbates the already stagnant economic atmosphere. All is not, however, negative, for this stagnant economic atmosphere does not imply a deteriorated social environment, for in a number of cases family, ethnic, and religious ties in the local community remain powerful cohesive forces.

ECONOMIC CONTROL

Decisions concerning the location of capital investments are made by the owners of capital. Thus, the pattern of the location of economic activities among the major urban regions of North America is the product of decisions made over a long period of time by entrepreneurs and corporations who either have, or can obtain, money capital to invest in the various facilities required for production. An examination of the outcome of these decisions involves, therefore, consideration of the way these decisions may have changed over the decades, and some discussion of the purpose of ownership. There are a number of approaches to these issues, but the most interesting probably involve (1) an outline of the general way in which locational interests have changed over the past 200 years and, most importantly, since 1920; and (2) a discussion of ownership and control in terms of class interests. These are interesting approaches because, as will become apparent, they offer a different perspective on changes in growth among North American urban systems from those discussed previously in this chapter.

Urban Growth and Location During Major Eras

During the mercantile era (1780/1840), economic activity which involved mostly trade, ship repair and refitting, and some small-scale manufacture of furniture and iron-products, occurred mostly in the port cities of the east coast. The population size of the leading cities of the time was quite small (Table 3.2), and all except Cincinnati and Albany are ports directly concerned with European trade. Cincinnati acted as the major service center and outlet from the rich Ohio valley down the Ohio and Mississippi rivers to New Orleans. Albany served as a major point of transshipment from the Hudson River and New York city to the area surrounding the lower Great Lakes. The mercantile era, therefore, witnessed the establishment of a number of small urban centers which served to protect the interests of the merchants and those involved with overseas trade. Capital investments were, therefore, directed towards those locations which provided good access to the agriculture, furs, and forests of the hinterland, and which were also good sites for sea trade.

A massive transformation occurred in North American urban development during the 1840/1890 national industrial era. The elements of this transformation involve the binding of the continent by the laces of the railroad, the realization of the extent of the natural resources, and the widespread development of manufacturing in the U.S. under the protection of tariff barriers. The financial basis for this development occurred through the money market in New York city, which had gained control of a massive hinterland through the construction of the Erie Canal (completed to Buffalo by 1825) and an extensive railroad network. In a similar manner, Philadelphia and Baltimore extended their control over large sections of the coal mining areas of Appalachian and the southern section of the middle-west. The result was that by 1890 a few large cities in the U.S. east coast (Table 3.2) had gained control of the import and export trade of the northeast and middle-west, became the centers of financing for the U.S., and also centers of manufacturing.

This latter aspect is a most important feature of urban development during this era for the factories of the big east coast cities, and also those of the service centers of the hinterland (Chicago, Cincinnati, and St. Louis), provided much of the basic employment of the urban regions. The cities began to grow large during this era because the factories provided jobs, and the output, whether it be in the form of textiles, farm machinery, or food products, was in great demand in a nation that was growing rapidly in wealth. The operators of the factories tended to be individual entrepreneurs who often ran their businesses as if they were personal fiefdoms. Control of the economic system was, therefore, concentrated in the sense of the location of finance capital (New York, Philadelphia, Baltimore, and Boston), but quite diffuse with respect to the number of entrepreneurs. It is interesting to notice that the major cities of the Windsor–Quebec City region languished by comparison during this era, for the economy of the Dominion (established in 1867) was still that of a British colony.

The early corporate era (1890/1940) witnessed a tremendous increase in the number of large metropolitan areas of half a million or more. During this period, the general structure of the diffused nature of single person or family entrepreneural control of manufacturing shifted to one of corporate control. Manufacturing concerns became massive with the development of the assembly line, and companies sought to integrate their productive capacity both horizontally and vertically. The large cities of the east coast continued to expand rapidly,

Table 3.2. Change in the North American urban system[a] (population in thousands).

1830/31	1870/71	1920/21	1970/71
New York (202.6)	New York (942.3)	New York (5260.0)	New York (9974)
Philadelphia (161.4)	Philadelphia (674.0)	Chicago (2701.7)	Los Angeles (7042)
Baltimore (80.6)	*Brooklyn* (396.1)	Philadelphia (1823.8)	Chicago (6978)
Boston (61.4)	*St. Louis* (310.8)	*Detroit* (993.7)	Philadelphia (4824)
New Orleans (46.3)	*Chicago* (299.0)	*Cleveland* (796.8)	Detroit (4435)
Quebec (27.7)	Baltimore (267.4)	St. Louis (772.9)	Boston (3376)
Montreal (27.0)	Boston (250.5)	Boston (748.0)	San Francisco (3109)
Cincinnati (24.8)	Cincinnati (216.2)	Baltimore (733.8)	Washington (2909)
Albany (24.2)	New Orleans (191.4)	Montreal (618.5)	Montreal (2587)
Washington (18.8)	*San Francisco* (149.5)	*Pittsburgh* (588.3)	*Nassau–Suffolk* (2556)
	Buffalo (117.7)	*Los Angeles* (576.7)	Toronto (2465.1)
	Washington (109.2)	*Toronto* (521.9)	St. Louis (2410)
	Montreal (107.2)	Buffalo (506.8)	Pittsburgh (2401)
	Newark (105.1)	San Francisco (506.7)	*Dallas–Fort Worth* (2378)
	Louisville (100.1)	*Milwaukee* (457.1)	Baltimore (2071)
		Washington (437.6)	Cleveland (2064)
		Newark (414.5)	Newark (2057)
		Cincinnati (401.2)	*Houston* (1999)
		Minneapolis (380.6)	Minn.–St. Paul (1965)
		Kansas City (324.4)	Atlanta (1596)
			Seattle (1425)
			Anaheim (1421)
			Milwaukee (1404)
			Cincinnati (1385)
			San Diego (1358)

[a]Cities in italics are additions to the lists of major cities in the different eras.

71

particularly New York which established itself as the center for the raising of finance capital in North America. Growth during the early part of this era was also fuelled by the millions of immigrants to the U.S. who provided an abundant supply of cheap labor.

Of particular importance during this era is the rapid growth of Chicago, Detroit, Cleveland, and Pittsburgh in the lower Great Lakes urban region; Montreal and Toronto in the Windsor–Quebec City area; and Los Angeles and San Francisco in California. In the case of the lower Great Lakes region, the growth of the metropolises in this area is in large part the result of heavy industry, such as iron, steel, and machinery in Pittsburgh, petrochemicals and iron and steel in Cleveland, and automobiles in Detroit. The headquarters of the major corporations that controlled most of the production were also located in these cities, and as other cities grew they sought to maintain their dominance by restrictive practices (such as the Pittsburgh-plus basing point system). On the west coast, San Francisco and Los Angeles also became established during the era as twin focii in the developing California urban system. The growth of these cities can also be interpreted from the economic control perspective for they effectively dominated the financing of agriculture and controlled trade within the region.

The 1890/1940 era is also particularly important in the development of the Canadian urban system. Montreal, and to a lesser extent Toronto, had become the financial capital of the nation, and the system of branch banking across the nation resulted in a few banks, with headquarter offices in these cities, dominating investments in the country. Furthermore, both Toronto and Montreal had promoted the development of a rail transport system which focussed upon them. Growth was also stimulated by World War I, for during this preiod manufacturing imports from Britain sharply diminished, and Canada began to foster the development of its own industries. These were established in the Monteral and Oshawa-Toronto-Hamilton areas. An interesting aspect of this manufacturing development is that as soon as a number of the manufacturing concerns reached a reasonable size they were absorbed by similar, but much larger, U.S. or British corporations. Also, a number of the plants established in the region were direct offshoots of larger American or European concerns.

During the present advanced corporate era (1940/1990?) there has been a shift in types of economic activities that predominate in the North American economy. The change is characterized most generally in the shift in emphasis from the products of "heavy" manufacturing to those of "light" manufacturing. This shift in emphasis has been accompanied by a change in the organization of economic activity from control via single industry national corporations to control through multi-industry multi-national corporations. As far as economic control is concerned, there are two important implications of these changes. The first is that these large corporations have interests in a wide variety of economic activities, possibly ranging from the manufacture of films for television to the smelting of base metals, and they are quite prepared to allow a portion of their assest to depreciate (as a tax loss) while other interests expand in profitability. The capital intensive heavy industries are particularly useful for tax-loss purposes of these kinds, and if these industries are located in particular urban regions, then the region tends to suffer from a lack of reinvestment.

The second implication is more specifically geographical for most of the large corporations are multi-locational. While the headquarter offices of the holding company may be located in New York, or Chicago, the many different components of the company are spread in cities around the continent and in different parts of the world. Thus, the corporation does not have an identity with a particular city or urban region, and is quite prepared to establish a plant in whatever location offers the best advantage. These advantages may be in the form of local or state tax breaks, a more attractive climate, or a more amenable political situation. The corporation may also seek to avoid locating plants in places where there may be racial or safety problems. The large corporation may, therefore, tend to help create economic stagnation in certain areas, and avoid locations where there seem to be complex social problems.

Along with these shifts from heavy to light manufacturing, and from the single-industry to the multi-industry corporation, has been a tremendous increase in the impact of federal government expenditures (particularly in the U.S.) on the economies of the different urban regions. On the surface, it would seem that the direction of these expenditures has been biased towards certain regions, and the reasons for this bias are quite complex. There is no doubt the political clout created by the seniority system in the federal government has played a role in the direction of considerable disbursements to the south, and it could be argued that the desire by the military establishment for prospective residential locations in pleasant climates might also have played a part in the locational decisions.

Class Interests and Differential Urban Growth

It may also be argued that the recent more rapid growth of some southern and western urban regions, and the slower growth of the Bosnywash and lower Great Lakes urban regions, can be explained in the context of the struggle between classes that is inherent to the capitalist economic system.[10] Comprehension of this argument requires an understanding of the difference between *quantitative* and *qualitative* efficiency in the production processes that take place within the urban areas of capitalist society. Briefly, a production process is quantitatively efficient if it generates the greatest physical output from a given quantity of physical inputs, whereas a production process is qualitatively efficient in a capitalist society if it maximizes the ability of the organizers and controllers of capital (the ruling classes) to dominate all the social processes of production. Thus, the objective of the organizers and controllers of capital is to generate a production process which best permits the maximization of qualitative efficiency subject to the constraint that these processes are also reasonably quantitatively efficient.

As a consequence, the urban regions of the south and west may be growing faster than those of the lower Great Lakes and Bosnywash urban regions because qualitative efficiency, along with a reasonable level of quantitative efficiency, can now be maximized more easily in these areas. Generally, the older cities of the east and middle-west consist of a legal central city which is now controlled politically by working class and minority interests, and suburbs which are fragmented and more easily dominated by capitalist interests. By contrast, the newer cities of the south and west tend to have avoided the legal city and fragmented suburb situation by annexation. Thus the working class and poor who reside in the inner portions of these cities can be dominated politically by generally middle- and upper-class interests who live separately from the poor and disadvantaged, but in the same political entity.

This advantageous situation is enhanced by the traditionally different political philosophy of the regions in which the more rapidly growing cities are found. Lupsha and Siembieda[11] comment that, in the south and parts of the west, the elected political elites have traditionally believed that many public services are beyond the obligations of society at large. Furthermore, there is some doubt that many southern and western politicians believe in equality of opportunity, and there certainly is little belief in the principle of equality of result. By contrast, many states in the lower Great Lakes and Bosnywash areas have substantial support for political philosophies supporting equal opportunity and a monitoring of the results. Thus, the shift of public and private capital investments, the establishment of new industries, and the growth of attractive recreational amenities in the "sunbelt" area are, according to this particular perspective, merely a continuation of the attempt by the middle and upper classes, and the organizers of capital to retain the economic control they were losing in the older urban regions.

One of the most important conclusions to be reached from an analysis of these various explanations for the shift in population growth among the major regions is that no one hypothesis explains *all* the different growth and stagnation situations that exist. The various growth experiences are far too complicated for any one explanation to be generally applicable. Therefore, the various public policy issues require a number of approaches. There is, however, one common thread that occurs in the discussions of public policy, and this relates to the power of the state to take a more active role in balancing growth and the availability of economic opportunities among the major urban regions. This particular role cannot be ignored, and neither can the responsibility for ignoring the results of past allocations of public monies. The role of government in generating or depressing economic growth is discussed in greater detail in the ensuing chapter.

NOTES

[1] D. C. Perry and A. J. Watkins, "Regional Change and the Impact of Uneven Urban Development" in D. C. Perry and A. J. Watkins (eds.), *The Rise of the Sunbelt Cities* (Beverly Hills, Calif.: Sage Publications, Urban Affairs Annual Reviews, Vol. 14, 1977).

[2] P. S. Lande and P. Gordon, "Regional Growth in the United States: A Re-examination of the Neoclassical Model," *Journal of Regional Science*, Vol. 17, No. 1 (1977), pp. 61–69.

[3] V. R. Fuchs, *Changes in the Location of Manufacturing in the United States Since 1929* (New Haven: Yale University Press, 1962).

[4] R. E. Lonsdale and C. E. Browning, "Rural-Urban Locational Preferences for Southern Manufacturers," *Annals of the Association of American Geographers*, Vol. 61 (1971), pp. 255–268.

[5] G. Peterson and T. Muller, "The Regional Impact of Federal Tax and Spending Policies" in *Alternatives to Confrontation: A National Policy Toward Economic Development* (Lexington: Saxon House/Lexington Books, 1979) (forthcoming).

[6] D. P. Moynihan, "The Politics and Economics of Regional Growth," *The Public Interest*, Vol. 51, (Spring, 1978), pp. 3-21.

[7] Nourse, H. O., "Equivalence of Central Place and Economic Base Theories of Urban Growth," *Journal of Urban Economics*, Vol. 5 (1978), pp. 543-549.

[8] A. Pred, "Industrialization, Initial Advantage, and American Metropolitan Growth," *Geographical Review*, Vol. 55 (1965), pp. 158-185.

[9] E. Rust, *No Growth Impacts on Metropolitan Areas* (Lexington, Mass.: Heath, 1975).

[10] D. M. Gordon, "Class Struggle and the Stages of American Urban Development" in D. C. Perry and A. J. Watkins (eds.), *The Rise of the Sunbelt Cities* (Beverly Hills, Calif.: Sage Publications, Urban Affairs Annual Reviews, Vol. 14, 1977, pp. 55-82).

[11] P. A. Lupsha and W. J. Siembieda, "The Poverty of Public Services in the Land of Plenty: An Analysis and Interpretation" in D. C. Perry and A. J. Watkins (eds.), *The Rise of the Sunbelt Cities* (Beverly Hills, Calif.: Sage Publications, Urban Affairs Annual Reviews, Vol. 14, 1977).

Chapter 4

Issues arising from macro-urban development

The trend toward the development of major urban regions, and the differential growth patterns among them and between them and the rest of continental North America, gives rise to a number of issues that are of particular interest in the area of public policy. These issues can be regarded broadly as involving matters related to demography, the location of economic activities and people, the organization of the metropolises within the urban regions, and the consumption of rural land for urban purposes. The specific focus of the discussion of each of these concerns is the role that the state has played, or can play, in the creation and resolution of the particular issues. The term "state" is used in a general sense, applying to national, state or provincial, and local governments of different kinds. At the outset, it must, of course, be recognized that the topic to be covered is quite broad and that any one of the issues, and the impact of any one particular level of government, can be examined in much greater detail. Nevertheless, an outline of the general issues provides a useful perspective from which to gauge the various public policy responses.

DEMOGRAPHIC ISSUES

Some of the most important trends underlying the different growth experiences of the major urban regions concern demographic changes in the North American population. The demographic changes involve changing rates of natural increase, migration patterns within the U.S. and Canada, and volumes of immigration as well as the destinations of the immigrants. In general, the total volume of population increase in North America has been decreasing since the mid 1960s, and it now appears quite likely that the decennial increase for the 1970s will be less than 10%, a percentage only slightly in excess of that experienced during the depression years in the decade of the 1930s. The factors influencing this decline are, however, somewhat different, for in the 1930s they were economic, whereas in the 1970s they are largely related to life-style preferences.

Changing Rates of Natural Increase

The total increase in population at any time period is made up of the natural increase and the increase resulting from net immigration. The natural increase is the product of the number of births less the number of deaths, and fluctuations in the rate of natural increase are, as a consequence, related to trends in these two components. The chief reason for the decrease in the rate of total population increase in the present decade is the decline in rate of natural increase. In the U.S., the rate of natural population increase has declined from 1.6% per annum in the late 1950s to less than 0.6% per annum in the mid 1970s. Similarly, in Canada, the rate of natural increase reached a high of 2.0% per annum in the 1950s, and declined to an average of about 0.7% per annum in the 1970s. This has been a dramatic fluctuation in the rate of natural increase within a 25-year period, and it has had enormous repercussions in many areas of public policy.

The reason for the decline in rate of natural increase is the decline in the birthrate. At the height of the "baby boom" in the late 1950s, the birthrate in both Canada and the U.S. was over 25 births per thousand population. By the mid 1970s the birthrate in both countries had decreased to 15-16 births per thousand population, and appears to be fluctuating at around that level. The slight increase in birthrate experienced in the latter part of the 1970s appears to be related to the large number of females (products of the "baby boom") who have reached child-bearing age, and is not due to an increase in the fertility rate (the number of births per woman of child bearing age). In fact, the number of births per woman appears to be continuing to decrease, and is approaching a figure of 2.1 births per woman of child bearing age, or zero population growth.

The impact of this "baby bust" on the rate of natural increase has been offset to a limited degree by a decline in the death rate. In both Canada and the U.S., death rates have been decreasing fairly continuously throughout the present century, and this decline is related to the statistical base of the measure as well as the increasing length of life. If there are a large number of people in the younger age groups, then, almost regardless of the actual average length of life, the death rate will be low. For example, the death rate in Canada in 1971 was 7.3 per thousand population, and in the U.S. 9.4 per thousand. This difference is due more to the relatively larger number of younger people in the population of Canada at that time than the difference in the average length of life between the two countries. In fact, the average length of life in both countries has been increasing, and for children born in the late 1960s the male life expectancy is about 69 years and female expectancy 76 years. This represents an increase in life expectancy of

9 years for males and 14 years for females in a 40-year period. The implications of the increasing numbers of elderly in the population are, of course, quite far reaching.[1]

The result of the twin forces of the decline in the birthrate and the decrease in the death rate, which together comprise a decline in the rate of natural increase, is extremely important.[2] The apparent convergence to zero population growth will result in many more metropolitan areas experiencing population decreases, at the same time as an increase in the number of older people. Consequently, the proportion of the population that is elderly will increase and there will be a concomitant heavier load on urban services, a decrease in the relative number of children of school age, and an increase in the importance of internal migration and immigration as factors which might offset population decreases. Thus, there will be a strain on the ability of urban areas to manage situations involving declining numbers of people along with an aging population. These are situations that are now being faced by many central cities and a few metropolitan areas in the Bosnywash and lower Great Lakes urban regions, as well as Seattle and Los Angeles on the west coast.

Internal Migration

With rates of natural increase decreasing, internal migration plays an increasingly important role in determining rates of differential growth.[3] The effect of migration can be examined at a number of different geographic scales, and from the perspective of this monograph the most significant are (1) the flows between major regions, (2) the flows between large metropolitan and small and nonmetropolitan areas, and (3) net migration patterns between inner cities and outer cities. These three general patterns of population movement all have significant effects on the relative growth performances between the major urban regions and shifts within the regions. Although data is not available that is specific to the major urban regions as defined, there is sufficient information prepared on other geographic bases to make inferences concerning trends among and within the major urban regions.

General Patterns of Net-migration. The overall patterns of net-migration for large regions in North America for the 1965/66-1970/71 and 1970/71-1975/76 periods are as indicated in Figure 4.1. The Bosnywash urban region comprises much of the northeast; the lower Great Lakes and Ohio Valley major urban regions are contained within the north central area and spill over into a part of the northeast; the south consists of the Florida, urban south, and Gulf coast major urban regions; and a portion of the west comprises California and the Pacific northwest major urban regions. In Canada, the Windsor-Quebec City urban region lies within the provinces of Ontario and Quebec. It should be noted that Figure 4.1 is a cartogram with the areas of the countries and the large regions corresponding to the size of the populations contained within them. The widths of the arrows indicates the relative volumes of net migration.

The general pattern of net-migration flows in the 1965/1970 period is, in the U.S., to the west and to the south. In Canada, the predominant flows are also to the west, but the Ontario portion of the Windsor-Quebec City urban region is

(a)

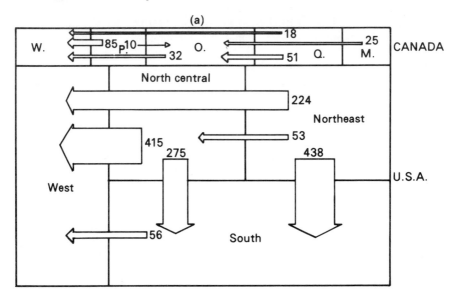

(b)

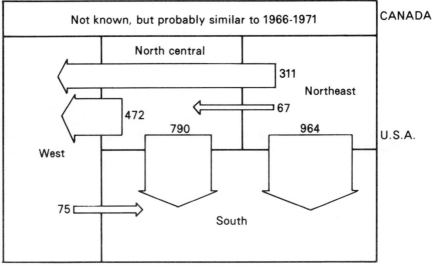

Fig. 4.1. Cartograms illustrating net-migration flows between large regions in the U.S. and Canada between (1) 1965/66 and 1970/71, and (b) 1970/71 and 1975/76. *Source*: U.S. data from Berry and Dahmann, 1977, p. 458.

also a destination of internal migrants. The net-migration pattern for the U.S. in the 1970/75 period is similar to the 1965/1970 period in terms of destinations, but quite different with respect to volumes. The total volume of new flows in the U.S. has almost doubled in the 10-year period, which was a time during which the rate of natural increase decreased by nearly one-third. Thus, the impact of net-migration on regional population growth rates is much greater than that indicated by the increase in volume. Furthermore, the direction of flows is, in the most recent period, clearly dominated by population shifts to the south, where the volume of net-migration has increased almost threefold, whereas the volume of flows to the west have increased only slightly.

The pattern of net-migration flows in Canada for the 1971/76 period is probably similar to that for 1966/1971,[4] though the volume to the west (which includes British Columbia and Alberta) is probably much greater as a result of the growth of the Alberta economy during the period. It is also quite likely that the volume of net-migration has increased slightly but nowhere near to the extent that it has in the U.S. Given similar reductions in the rate of natural increase, it is evident that the importance of internal migration as a determinant of differences in regional growth patterns in Canada has also increased dramatically between the 1960s and 1970s.

Metropolitan and Nonmetropolitan Migration Flows. One of the interesting features noted with respect to Table 2.15 has been the slight decline in proportion to the North American population found within the nine major urban regions in the last decade. The proportion increased fairly steadily up to 1970/71 but declined by nearly half a percentage point by 1975/76. Part of the reason for this is the increase in importance of the movement of people from metropolitan areas (which comprise most of the major urban regions) to nonmetropolitan areas, which for the most part lie outside the major urban regions. Although there has been a pattern of net out-migration from metropolitan areas (SMSAs and CMAs) for the past two decades, the rate of natural increase within metropolitan areas tended to mask this pattern until recent years. Now, with the decline in the rate of natural increase, the effect of this trend is becoming more evident.

The volumes involved in the metropolitan/nonmetropolitan pattern of migration flows is indicated in Figure 4.2. The area of the circle representing the SMSAs in the U.S. is a little more than twice that of the nonmetropolitan circle in accordance with the difference in population size between the two categories. There are a number of important elements to notice from this diagram. First, 396,000 more people left metropolitan areas for nonmetropolitan areas, a net out-migration that stands in contrast to the historical experience over two centuries. Second, a large volume of people moved between nonmetropolitan counties, indicating probably a continued search for a more rural environment. Finally, the largest volume of all moved among SMSAs, a flow of considerable interest as a large portion of this undoubtedly represents migration from metropolitan areas in the Bosnywash and lower Great Lakes urban regions to those urban regions in the south and west, and also movements to SMSAs lying beyond the major urban regions (such as Dallas–Ft. Worth, Denver, Phoenix, and Tucson). Bourne[5] notes similar inter-CMA moves in the 1970s in Canada, where the largest

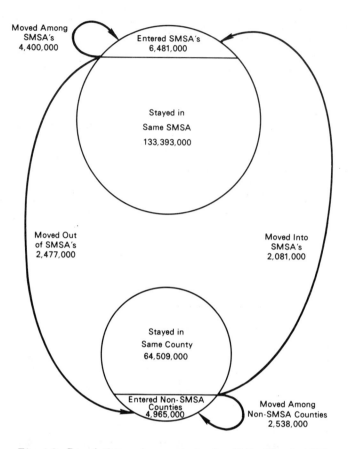

Fig. 4.2. Population movements in the U.S., March 1975 to March 1976. *Source*: U.S. Bureau of the Census, *Current Population Reports*, P-20, No. 305, "Geographic Mobility: March 1975 to March 1976.

metropolitan areas (Toronto, Montreal, and Vancouver) have grown less than some smaller CMAs, such as Calgary, Edmonton, or Kitchener–Waterloo.

Inner-city/Outer-city Migration. One of the continued trends within urban regions, that is in part exemplified by metropolitan-nonmetropolitan migration patterns, is the decentralization of population from the inner or central city to the suburbs or outer-city. This is in part exemplified by the metropolitan-nonmetropolitan moves because many of the nonmetropolitan moves represent shifts to counties immediately adjacent to SMSAs and CMAs. The general pattern of population shifts that has occurred within SMSAs is indicated in Figure 4.3, where the greatest volume of net-migration between 1970 and 1975 involved movements from central cities to suburban areas. This movement involved a net loss from the central cities of nearly 6 million people alone, and to this must be added the 1.1 million who moved from the central cities to nonmetropolitan areas. The impact of this decentralization is a decline in the taxable base of the inner cities, a racially divided metropolis when the majority of the population that remains in the inner city is of a particular minority, and an increased consumption of rural land for urban purposes.

Although all the larger metropolises in the major urban regions of Canada increased in population between 1971 and 1976, there has been a similar decline in the population of the central cities. In Table 4.1, those metropolises with a population of greater than 500,000, located in the major urban regions, have been listed along with the proportion of their population contained in the central city portion of the CMA in 1971 and 1976. All of these large metropolises have experienced actual declines in central city population, and the largest metropolises in particular have experienced significant decreases in the proportion

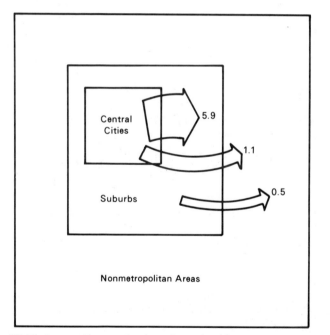

Note: Width of arrows is proportional to volume of net flows among the three areas

Fig. 4.3. Net residential flows (in millions) between the inner city, outer city, and nonmetropolitan areas in the U.S., 1970/75. *Source*: U.S. Bureau of the Census, *Current Population Reports*, P-20, No. 285, "Mobility of the Population of the United States: March 1970 to March 1975," in Berry and Dahmann, 1977, p. 460.

Table 4.1. Central city population as a percentage of total metropolitan area population, selected Canadian CMAs, 1976 and 1971.

CMA	1976 (%)	1971 (%)	Change in central city population
Montreal	38	44	−154,315
Toronto	22	27	−101,615
Vancouver	35	39	−29,735
Ottawa–Hull	52	59	−16,673
Quebec City	33	37	−13,874
Hamilton	59	61	−328

of their CMA population (constant boundaries) found in the central city. The implications of this decentralization of population within metropolitan areas is similar to that for the U.S. with the one exception that there is not the same racial division as a consequence.

The Role of Immigration

As the rate of natural increase decreases, the volume of immigration from outside Canada, and outside the U.S., plays an increasing important role in influencing the total increase. During the 1960s, the average annual net immigration to Canada was about 77,000 persons per year, and to the U.S. almost 400,000 per year. Thus, taking into account the tenfold difference between the Canadian and U.S. total populations, immigration is nearly twice as significant in the Canadian situation as in the U.S. The destination of immigrants within Canada has been primarily to southern Ontario (about 50%), which really means the area around Toronto; Quebec (20%), which means Montreal; and British Columbia (30%), which means Vancouver.[6] During the 1970s it is estimated that the volume of net immigration is about 60,000 per year, with a much smaller proportion selecting residential locations in the Province of Quebec, and a significant number selecting Edmonton and Calgary in Alberta. The generally lower volume of immigration that is expected to occur through the 1980s, and the choice by the immigrants of a limited number of locations, will obviously have a significant influence on differences in metropolitan growth.

In the U.S., the annual recorded volume of immigration in the 1970s has been similar to that in the 1960s, but the actual number is probably twice that contained in the census. The estimates vary enormously, but there is anywhere between 5 and 10 million illegal residents in the U.S., most of whom enter across the U.S.-Mexico border. The destinations of the legal and illegal immigrants are primarily the major metropolitan areas of the southern and California urban regions, and New York City. Given the high volume of illegal immigrants involved, and the generally higher fertility rates of Mexican-Americans, it is evident that this component of U.S. demography will exert a significant impact on differential growth rates in the future. It is quite likely that population increases in the Sunbelt cities (California and the south) have been underestimated in the 1970s; and New York City, with an illegal alien population of 0.5–2.0 million, may have actually increased rather than decreased in population.

One feature of the destination of immigrants in both Canada and the U.S. that needs to be emphasized is that many inevitably are found in the inner cities. Though not all immigrants are poor, many are, and financial difficulties are often compounded by linguistic and cultural differences. The inner city has a residue of older buildings which provide low-cost housing (in absolute terms), and the vacuum created by departing whites (and a few blacks) leaves neighborhoods which can be occupied by the new ethnic groups. There is little doubt, for example, that large population declines in the central cities of the bigger Canadian metropolises would have been experienced during the 1960s were it not for the large volume of Italian and Portuguese immigrants who came to the country during the period. In the U.S., the inner cities of some metropolitan areas may contain many more people than that recorded by the census, which implies that some central cities are receiving less money than they should from such schemes as revenue sharing which are based on population counts.

Demographic Issues and Public Policy

The extent to which public policy in North America can have a direct influence on demographic issues is quite limited. For example, the rate of natural increase is largely a product of the fertility rate, and it is not at all clear how or why the fertility rate has fluctuated the way it has over the past 30 years. Furthermore, given the different pressures for and against zero population growth, it would be difficult to decide what rate of natural increase is desirable. Other countries have attempted to influence the fertility rate with child subsidies (up to a certain number of children), and, in North America, the development of support systems (such as day care, etc.) for parents might influence the decision to have children.

Governments have attempted to influence internal migration patterns by various regional development programs aimed at improving economic and social conditions and providing employment opportunities in less developed parts of the continent. The evidence, however, tends to suggest that economic opportunities, such as higher incomes or greater possibilities for employment, are less of an influence on internal migration patterns than is generally supposed.[7] Potential migrants appear to be more influenced by social factors and features of the physical environment, and these are aspects that are difficult to alter through public policy actions. Much of the movement of population to the Florida and California urban regions is, for example, related directly to environmental conditions, and the only way that migration patterns of this type can be "controlled" via public policy mechanisms is through government limitations on the freedom of movement, a procedure which is alien to the North American political systems. This is, however, being attempted by states and provinces which require that vacancies in the public service and some privately owned industries (such as construction) be filled by residences of the state or province.

Perhaps the only demographic issue that can be influenced directly by public policy is the volume of immigration and, to a much lesser degree, the destination of immigrants. The Canadian federal government is now attempting to adjust the flow of immigrants to national manpower needs, and predictions through the 1980s suggest an annual volume of net immigration of about 60,000 per year, though net immigration in 1978 dropped to 30,000. There has also been a limited attempt to influence the destination of immigrants, and the 1978 Federal–Quebec agreement with respect to French-language immigrants portends further developments in this area. But, once an immigrant is inside a country, there is no control whatsoever on the ultimate place of residence.

In the U.S., the volume of legal immigration is fixed at about 400,000 per year, but, as indicated previously, with illegal immigration probably doubling this figure, it is evident that the public policy decision is, in effect, to allow the growth of an "underclass" of workers who do not have the advantages of legal residence. This "policy" would appear to be supported by big farm, industrial, and recreational (hotel) interests who require cheap labor, as well as the bulk of the population who can take advantage of the lower cost services that are provided.

ISSUES ARISING FROM GOVERNMENTAL INFLUENCES ON THE LOCATION OF ECONOMIC ACTIVITIES AND PEOPLE

Although there have been no clearly articulated policies related to national urban development in North America, there has been the creation of "accidental" urban policies[8] through a variety of different programs each aimed at alleviating particular problems. Though it would be impossible to cover all of these, it is instructive to examine some of the urban impacts of federal policies in the two countries involved with respect to transport, housing, the location of defense facilities, and the location of federal civilian employment. In the U.S., a report from the Rand Corporation, (*The Urban Impact of Federal Policies*), suggests that federal programs in these areas may have had a greater impact than all other post-1945 policies combined.[9]

Transport and Urban Development

One of the major influences on the decentralization of population within metropolises and the major urban regions, and the greater growth of population and economic activities in the south and west, has been the construction of limited access highway systems in the U.S., and, to a lesser degree, in Canada (Fig. 4.4). The construction of the high-capacity limited access Interstate Highway System in the U.S. in the late 1950s, 1960s, and early 1970s, which was originally designed to link all urban places with a population of 50,000 or more, has fostered the dominance of the trucking industry and has contributed to the reduction in importance of the railroad as a continental carrier of goods.

As far as urbanization is concerned, the impact of the limited-access four-lane highway has been felt at both the metropolitan and continental levels. At the

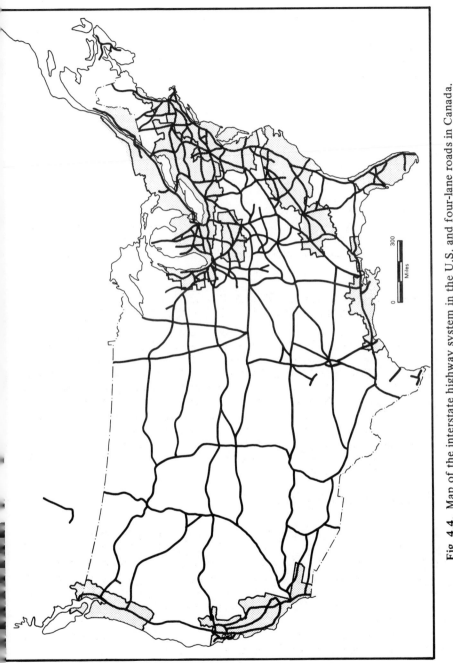

Fig. 4.4. Map of the interstate highway system in the U.S. and four-lane roads in Canada.

metropolitan level, the construction of such highway systems has accelerated the decentralization of population and manufacturing activities. At the continental level, the system of high-speed highways provides greater coverage than the railroad network, and is more flexible from the point of view of the user. As a consequence, not only does the highway system make it possible for business activities to locate in metropolitan areas that are poorly served by rail transport, it also facilitates the migration of people. Now, a person or family can move itself by renting the appropriate haulage facilities and driving, in a short space of time, to wherever they wish to go. The interstate system in effect "opened up" the south and west to the inhabitants of the metropolises around the lower Great Lakes and Bosnywash major urban regions. Particularly noticeable in Figure 4.4 are the number of highways focussing on the larger metropolises within the major urban regions, and the equally high level of accessibility generated by the number of highways focussing on the larger metropolises (such as Dallas–Ft. Worth, St. Louis, Kansas City, Denver, etc.) lying beyond the major urban regions.

Although there is not the same extensive limited-access highway system in the Canadian portion of the axis, decentralization within the larger metropolises has been facilitated by the construction of freeways, and the entire length of the Windsor–Quebec City region is served by a four-lane limited-access road. This highway system has become the "main street" of central Canada, the artery along which goods and people can move with ease and rapidity between the metropolises, towns, and cities within the region. The connection of this highway with the U.S. interstate system through Detroit has reinforced the economic ties of southern Ontario with the lower Great Lakes urban region. Similarly the highway linkage south from Montreal to the Bosnywash urban region has reinforced the weaker economic linkages that exist between southern Quebec and the New York area.

Housing

The federal governments of North America have, for the past four decades, been involved, both directly and indirectly, with the stimulation of housing construction. The policies that have been developed have been concerned with (1) providing a greater supply of better quality housing, (2) the "renewal" of some sections of inner cities, (3) the provision of some housing for the poor and elderly, and (4) the use of housing construction to stimulate the economy in times of recession.[10] All of the programs established to achieve these different purposes have had the effect of decentralizing the population and encouraging the spread of low density suburbs, subsidizing home ownership among the middle and upper classes, and, in the U.S., fostering the segregation of the population according to color. These are quite general conclusions, and some examples may indicate the basis for them.

The Federal Housing Administration in the U.S. was established in the mid 1930s to help stimulate the economy by promoting the construction of *new* housing. To achieve this purpose, and at the same time provide better quality housing for the population at large, the FHA was directed to establish a mortgage insurance program for the *lenders* of mortgage money. This was designed to increase the flow of money available for borrowers who wished to enter the housing market as well as hold interest rates to the lowest level possible. The Central Mortgage and Housing Corporation was established in 1945 in Canada, and one of its functions was similar to that described for the FHA. The result was, after 1945 in the U.S. and after 1952 in Canada (the Canadian post-war recovery was slower than that of the U.S.), a massive increase in the volume of new housing that had to be built on new urban land, which was generally available in large quantities only at the periphery of cities. These two agencies thus facilitated the construction of suburbs and the decentralization of the urban population.

The social impact of the housing insurance schemes has been equally as significant as the impact on population decentralization. In the first place, the borrowers had to have a certain minimum annual income, usually that defining the lower end of the "middle class" income range, and so the section of the North American population most able to take advantage of the low interest, low down payment, insured loans were the middle and upper classes. Hence the insured loan program had the effect of subsidizing capital transfers to the middle and upper classes, and also reinforced the spatial separation of the middle and upper income groups at the periphery of cities from the generally lower income groups in the more central locations. Along with this, in the U.S., the lending program also accentuated spatial separation according to race, for the lending institutions were a vital link in the complex web of discriminatory practices that prevented even those blacks that qualified from participating. For example, between 1960 and 1970 the population of N.W. Cook County (suburban Chicago) increased by 222,800 people, but of this number less than 200 were blacks.

Thus, not only has the proportion of the population of metropolitan areas contained in the central city decreased in nearly all cases in the large metropolises of the major urban regions (Tables 4.1 and 4.2), but the proportion of the population that is nonwhite has also increased in U.S. cities, and the population residing in the central cities is generally poorer than that in the suburbs (Table 4.2). These characteristics are particularly relevant with respect to the metropolises of the Bosnywash and lower Great Lakes urban regions. The maps of income by census tract in Ray[11] for Canadian metropolises also indicate that lower income families reside in the central part of cities and wealthier families in the suburbs; this can be regarded as, in large part, the indirect outcome of housing policies.

The affect of housing policies on the redistribution of population towards nonmetropolitan areas of the U.S. has been detailed by Beaton and Cox.[12] They argue that the Housing and Community Development Act of 1974, which was designed to provide federal grant money to counties and municipalities for the improvement of basic public infrastructure (such as sewage and water systems), as implemented by HUD, actually encourages extensive scattered suburban-tract type developments in rural America. This is because the indicators developed by HUD, for the determination of the extent of need for federal grant money provided through the Act, provide a misleading set of information concerning actual need. Furthermore, Beaton and Cox contend that the scattered urbanization of rural areas, which is fostered by this program, is also encouraged by the Department of Agriculture's Rural Development Act of 1972 and the Federal

Table 4.2. Some measures of differences between central cities and suburbs for large metropolises in the major urban regions of the U.S.

Region and SMSA	City	Population in city (%)		Nonwhite in city (%)		Per capita income Ratio	Local government (N)
		1973	1960	1970	1960	1973	
Bosnywash	New York	67	72	23.5	14.7	.84	538
	Philadelphia	38	46	34.4	26.7	.83	852
	Boston	22	26	17.6	9.8	.79	147
	Washington, D.C.	24	36	72.4	54.8	.84	90
	Baltimore	41	52	47.0	35.0	.79	29
	Newark	19	23	56.0	34.4	.56	207
	Hartford	22	29	29.2	15.5	.72	68
	Providence	35	43	5.6	3.6	.97	84
	Bridgeport	38	46	17.3	9.9	.78	27
	Norfolk	56	72	34.9	28.6	.92	10
	Jersey City	42	45	22.2	13.5	.91	33
	Richmond	44	50	42.6	42.0	.90	7
Lower Great Lakes	Chicago	45	47	34.4	23.6	.80	1,172
	Detroit	33	44	44.5	29.2	.80	241
	Pittsburgh	20	25	20.7	16.8	.91	698
	Milwaukee	48	57	15.6	8.9	.82	149
	Buffalo	31	40	21.3	13.8	.85	142
	Rochester	31	43	17.6	7.6	.80	198
	Albany	33	42	8.6	5.5	.93	216
	Toledo	53	50	14.3	12.7	.86	137
	Akron	38	47	17.8	13.1	.95	98
	Syracuse	28	38	11.9	5.7	.96	182
	Gary	51	60	33.9	24.6	.87	129
	Grand Rapids	34	38	11.7	8.3	.92	93
	Youngstown	35	44	22.2	17.1	.87	107
	Flint	35	47	28.6	17.7	.94	95
California	Los Angeles	44	46	21.2	15.4	1.03	232
	San Francisco	32	41	32.7	15.0	.95	302
	Anaheim	29	40	3.7	1.4	.99	111
	San Diego	51	55	11.1	7.8	1.08	151
	San Bernardino	27	27	9.3	6.1	1.01	233
	San Jose	45	31	6.4	3.3	.80	75
	Sacramento	30	30	18.5	12.7	1.03	210
The urban South	Atlanta	30	47	51.6	38.4	.84	86
	Birmingham	39	47	42.2	39.7	.84	92
	Charlotte	63	65	30.6	28.0	1.22	20
Florida	Miami	25	31	23.4	22.6	.77	33
	Tampa	43	59	17.8	15.5	.93	45
	Jacksonville	100	44	24.3	23.4	–	9
Gulf shore	Houston	60	66	26.6	23.2	1.05	304
	New Orleans	52	69	45.5	37.4	.93	42
Ohio Valley	Cincinnati	30	39	23.1	21.8	.93	260
	Indianapolis	51	64	18.3	15.2	1.04	296
	Columbus	57	62	19.0	16.6	.81	128
	Dayton	25	36	30.9	21.9	.77	161
Pacific Northwest	Seattle	39	50	11.6	7.9	1.07	269
	Portland	35	45	7.8	5.6	.93	298
	Tacoma	38	45	9.3	5.3	.98	79

Source: Advisory Commission on Intergovernmental Relations (1977) *Trends in Metropolitan America*, Washington, D.C.: AC on IR.

Water Pollution Control Act of 1972. The combined effect of these programs is the stimulation of urban type developments in the nonmetropolitan parts of the country.

Effect of the Location of Defense Facilities and Federal Civilian Employment

In the examination of the economic base of the economic areas within the major urban regions, the nature of the impact of the location of federal defense facilities has already been mentioned. The location of these defense facilities, as revealed by the economic base data, appears to be disproportionately located in the southern and western major urban regions. Of the 18 economic areas that have a large portion of their economic base derived from defense employment, 16 are in the major urban regions of the south and west. The importance of these defense activities in some of the economic areas may, however, be overestimated, for though the direct impact may be substantial, the indirect impact (which results from the employment generated locally by expenditures from the defense facilities) in a number of instances may be quite limited. As a consequence, the multiplier effect of some of the defense activities on the local economies may be much less than in other areas. Nevertheless, there is no doubt that employment generated by the state in these activities has had a definite influence on urban growth.

Similarly, expenditures on civilian employment by the state also has a definite impact on urban growth. Washington, D.C. and Ottawa are cities that are based on federal government employment, and they have been among the fastest growing metropolises on the continent over the past two decades. Other economic areas where the location of employment in governmental activities has also generated urban growth are Quebec City, San Francisco, Sacramento, Albany, and Baltimore. The effect of governmental policies on regional variations in urban growth has been examined in terms of an explicit program by Markusen and Fastrup.[13] The particular program is the energy program as administered by the U.S. Department of Energy. Markusen and Fastrup[14] claim that the Department has ". . . let many of its huge research and development contracts to the same military-industrial complex that fuelled Sunbelt growth." In general, the energy initiatives involving coal-fired electricity generation, pipelines, the development of technology to rejuvenate declining oil fields, all involve massive transfers of capital to the Gulf coast and west. Similarly, there has been a large flow of capital to the Canadian west, particularly Alberta, as a result of Canadian federal energy policies, and Edmonton and Calgary are now Canada's fastest growing metropolises.

These few examples, and there are many others involving activities ranging from inner city renewal to regional development, all emphasize the way in which the state inadvertently establishes programs which create powerful forces affecting urban growth. The relating of the examples should in no way be construed as general criticism of the consequences of the programs on urbanization, for there is no intention of implying that growth, or decline, in one part of the continent is more acceptable, or less acceptable, than in others. It is, however, necessary to recognize that even in North America, where federal governments appear to have few policies with respect to national urban development, the various policies as enunciated, and programs as formulated, whether they be concerned with transport, housing, defense, or governmental activities, do have quite definite effects on national and local urban development.

METROPOLITAN ORGANIZATION

With the development of large metropolitan areas and the merging of metropolises one into the other, it is becoming apparent that one of the chief issues facing urban regions is that of efficient government and adequate levels of finance. The major urban regions consist of a myriad different municipalities, and while the responsibilities of these local governments have expanded greatly since 1920, the sources of finance and the structure of local government have not, in general, widened to a comparable extent. The range of administrative, service, and social activities undertaken by municipalities in North America in the 1970s is immense. Although larger municipalities tend to have assumed a wider range of responsibilities than smaller ones, a general outline of the activities normally undertaken by local governments with a population greater than 50,000 is as listed for the U.S. in Table 4.3. Although many of the headings in the table represent summaries of activities—e.g., sewerage and sanitation includes garbage collection and disposal; sewage collection, treatment, and disposal; and street cleaning—it is constructive to note that most of the activities are vitally important for day-to-day living.

Local Government Finance

The allocation of expenditures among the different activities is also listed in Table 4.3, along with the changing distribution of expenditures between 1965 and 1975. Even though local government budget allocations only change incrementally, there have been some significant shifts in priorities since 1965, and some of these shifts reflect a continued emphasis on matters of social concern as compared with the traditional interests of local government in the provision and maintenance of basic physical infrastructure and utilities. The items of expenditure receiving the largest proportionate increase in budgetary allocation are public welfare, health, and hospitals, categories that have been particularly subject to spiralling inflation in recent years. The largest decreases in expenditures are in areas having to do with highway construction and maintenance, utilities, housing, and urban renewal, the latter occurring largely as a result of increases in federal activities in these areas.

With the large increase in volume of expenditures in a 10-year period as indicated in Table 4.3, it is not surprising that national, state or provincial, and local governments are keen competitors for any kind of tax dollar. The federal governments of both the U.S. and Canada raise the vast bulk of their revenue from personal income taxes, payroll taxes, sales and excise taxes. They are able to impose

Table 4.3. Expenditures by municipalities in the U.S. in 1965 and 1975.

Activity	Expenditure (in billions of dollars)		Percentage		Comparative change
	1965	1975	1965	1975	1965/1975
Police protection	1.7	5.3	8.2	8.7	+6.1
Fire protection	1.1	2.9	5.3	4.8	−9.4
Highways	1.8	3.9	8.7	6.4	−26.4
Sewerage, etc.	1.8	5.2	8.7	8.6	−1.1
Public welfare	.9	3.8	4.3	6.4	+48.8
Education	2.5	7.2	12.1	11.9	−1.7
Libraries	.2	.6	1.0	1.0	0.0
Health and hospitals	1.1	3.6	5.3	6.0	+13.2
Parks and recreation	.8	2.3	3.9	3.8	−2.5
Housing and urban renewal	.7	1.8	3.4	3.0	−13.3
Airports	.2	.6	1.0	1.0	0.0
Administration	1.0	3.1	4.8	5.1	+6.3
Utilities	4.0	9.9	19.3	16.4	−15.0
Interest	.6	2.3	2.9	3.8	+31.0
Other	2.3	7.9	11.1	13.1	+18.0
Total	20.7	50.4	100.0	100.0	

Source: U.S. Bureau of the Census, *City Government Finances*, annual.

relatively high rates of taxation of these kinds because the respective national territories are under their jurisdiction. Many of the states, and all of the Canadian provinces, also raise revenue through income taxes, business and sales taxes, and other devices (such as lotteries). Smaller geographical units, such as municipalities, cannot take full advantage of these sources of revenue, either because they are not allowed to do so (as with income taxes), or because they are afraid to do so in an economic system in which business, people, and capital can move relatively freely among its various geographical parts.

As a consequence, municipalities raise or receive revenue from a variety of sources (Table 4.4) among which the most important are property taxes and direct transfers from state or provincial governments. In Canada, municipalities receive, on the average, between 80 and 85% of their revenue from property taxes and the various provincial governments; while in the U.S. property and state taxes account for just over half of the revenues, and local governments receive a significant amount of money in direct transfers from the federal government. The Canadian provincial-municipal and federal-municipal situation is quite different from that in the U.S., the implications of which will be discussed in greater length in the next chapter. One of the interesting contrasts is, however, that U.S. municipalities receive intergovernmental financial transfers from both

Table 4.4.   Sources of revenue received by municipalities in the
U.S. in 1965 and 1975.

Source	Amount received (in billions of dollars)		Percentage		Comparative change 1965/1975
	1965	1975	1965	1975	
State governments	2.8	13.1	13.8	21.9	+58.7
Local property taxes	6.5	13.1	32.0	21.9	−31.7
Local sales taxes	1.8	4.6	8.9	7.7	−13.4
Local licenses	1.0	3.5	4.9	5.9	+20.4
Local direct charges	3.1	9.1	15.3	15.3	0.0
Utility revenue	3.9	8.4	19.2	14.1	−26.6
Other (e.g., federal transfers)	1.2	7.9	5.9	13.2	+123.7
Total	20.3	59.7	100.0	100.0	

Source: U.S. Bureau of the Census, *Statistical Abstract of the United States*, 1977, table 483.

the states and federal government, whereas Canadian municipalities are directly dependent on provincial largesse.

Local Government Fragmentation

It is estimated that there were, in 1972, 78,269 different units of local government in the U.S.,[15] and of these 9,085 political jurisdictions occur within the 48 large SMSAs located within the defined 8 major urban regions (Table 4.2). These

Table 4.5.   Proliferation of units of local
government in the Windsor–Quebec City
major urban region, 1972.

Type of unit	Number
Counties	98
Municipalities and townships	1,827
School districts	920
Special districts (est.)	3,400
Total	6,245

Source: Yeates (1975), p. 267.

units of local government consist of counties, municipalities, townships (including New England towns), special districts or special purpose bodies, and school districts. Some idea of the extent of local government fragmentation within a major urban region is indicated in Table 4.5, in which it is estimated that there were more than 6,000 different types of units of local government in the area, for the service of about 12 million people. Of course, the majority of these units of local government were special purpose bodies, most of which have no power to raise revenue and are subordinate, in one way or another, to another political unit of local government.

Some of the special purpose bodies are, however, quite large and powerful. For example, the Toronto Transit Commission is large business enterprise which serves the entire metropolitan Toronto area with buses, rapid transit, streetcars, and commuter train services, and raises its revenue through user charges, bond issues, as well as receiving a share of tax revenues from the metropolitan and provincial governments in the form of subsidies. The largest and most powerful special purpose body in North America is, however, the Port of New York Authority, which controls port activities in two states, and also operates six airports, the World Trade Center, six interstate bridges and tunnels, and many other activities related to trade and transportation. One of the interesting features of these special purpose bodies, which involve schools, fire districts, police, health care, libraries, zoning, and the provision of public housing, is that in many cases the members of the governing boards are usually appointed by other elected officials.

The extent of fragmentation does, however, vary quite markedly between the different metropolitan areas (Table 4.2). In general, the newer metropolitan areas, such as those in the west and south, have fewer political units and simpler spatial patterns than the older ones in the northeast, and the complexity of urban government is related to population size. For example, in 1972 the 28 SMSAs in Table 4.2 having a population of more than 1 million have an average of 257 local government units of all kinds per SMSA, while the 20 SMSAs with a population of less than 1 million averaged only 94 per SMSA. The most prolific SMSA was Chicago with a total of over 1170 units, followed by Philadelphia, Pittsburgh, and New York. But, size is only a rough guide, for the SMSA of Los Angeles–Long Beach, which had a population of 7 million people in 1972, had only 232 local government units, and Baltimore, with a population of over 2 million, had only 29 local government units. In fact, every major central city, with the sole exception of Baltimore, shares its territory with at least one, and frequently several other, independent local governments.

Local Government Issues

Two main kinds of problems occur as a result of demands placed on, and the proliferation and fragmentation of, local governments. These are: (1) fiscal, involving issues related to the existing methods of financing local government activities; and (2) organizational, concerning the difficulties experienced in coordinating the various local government responsibilities within metropolitan areas. Although the second class of problems is often a result of the first, for, in order to raise funds local governments are forced into the pursuit of conflicting rather than cooperative policies, the two categories will be considered separately.

Fiscal Problems. The major problem arising from the fragmentation of local government structure is the tremendous disparity between revenue resources and expenditure needs among different local government units within urban areas. The segregation of resources and needs is most pronounced between the central cities and the suburbs, although not all suburban communities enjoy a favorable tax base. If per capita income is regarded as an indicator of ability to pay taxes, the per capita income ratio data for 1973 in Table 4.2 indicates that, in general, the per capita income level of the central cities is less than that for the suburbs. For example, the per capita income of inhabitants residing in the central city of Detroit in 1973 was 80% of that of inhabitants of the suburbs in the rest of the SMSA. The income disparity appears to be greatest in the larger cities of the Bosnywash, lower Great Lakes metropolises, and urban south major regions than elsewhere. Furthermore, trends indicate that the income disparity between the central cities and the suburbs is increasing.

This income disparity between the central cities and the suburbs is accentuated by a concomitant slower rate of increase in the taxable base of the central cities. In the previous section, the importance of the property tax as a source of revenue has been emphasized. The amount of taxable income that can be generated by a local government from this source depends upon the magnitude of the assessed property values within its jurisdiction. Data collected by the Advisory Commission on Intergovernmental Relations[16] indicates that the increase in the growth rate of assessed values for most central cities "is substantially below the growth rate in income for the same city."[17] Thus, not only have many of the larger central cities, particularly those outside the west and south, experienced a decline in population that can pay taxes, but they have also incurred a greater decline in their ability to raise revenue via the property tax. It is for this reason that financial transfers from the state or provincial governments, and federal government in the U.S., to metropolitan areas has been particularly important for the central cities.

But, even with these transfers, many central cities are finding it difficult to obtain funds sufficient to meet the demands of the inhabitants. Although some suburban communities are now beginning to experience similar levels of fiscal imbalance, it is the disparity between the central cities and the suburban municipalities that is one of the most iniquitous features in the contemporary spatial organization of metropolitan areas. The result is that a central city, such as New York City, has fallen into budgetary practices that have left it with a huge debt which has been incurred to cover not only capital costs, but operating costs as well. This is not just because of the city's welfare payments, benefits to the elderly, retirement costs, and wages paid to city employees, all of which are not excessive when compared with other major metropolitan areas, or its level of efficiency in delivery of comparable public services which tend to be equal to or better than many other older metropolitan areas.[18]

The surface cause of the financial problems of New York is the 542,000 jobs lost in the central city between 1969 and 1976, a rate of job loss that was twice that of the preceding 7-year period. For each job lost, the city loses between $651 and $1,035 in tax revenues, and if the jobs that disappeared during the 1970s were providing tax income for the city there would be no financial crisis. The real, or sub-surface, causes of the crisis are the forces that give rise to the migration of people and jobs from the central cities to the suburbs, nonmetropolitan parts of the urban regions, and to other parts of the nation. The forces that influence this decentralization process have been discussed previously.

Organizational Problems. The nature of most of the services provided within metropolitan regions, and the problems that local governments have to resolve, is such that they cannot be managed effectively by a large number of municipalities and other forms of government acting in isolation. This situation is exacerbated by the fact that many local governments within a metropolitan area actually compete with each other for acceptable tax yielding economic activities. The heavy reliance on the property tax forces local governments to meet increased costs, or to hold outlays to a reasonable level, by using their zoning powers for fiscal ends. Different types of land use demand different kinds of services, and, at the same time, are capable of making different sized contributions to the public purse. Thus, whereas commercial and light industrial activities, and high income families living in expensive homes, are often able to contribute in taxes two or three times the costs of services they require, residential property of moderate value pays only a fraction of the cost of public services it requires.

The problems arising from fragmented local government in metropolitan areas are most clearly revealed in the conflicting programs of service provision, especially those administered by the boards of special districts. These special districts often operate over wide areas (such as natural drainage areas, or entire metropolises), and can raise their own revenues through a variety of means such as bonds and user charges. Though the single-purpose nature of these activities has undoubted advantages, the lack of coordination often witnessed with other levels of local government can lead to severe problems. For example, the Port of New York Authority is responsible for the construction of the twin-tower World Trade Center in New York City, and by labeling it a port facility the Authority is able to avoid payment of about $50 million annually in property and other taxes to the city.[19] This tax exemption persists despite the contention that many of the users of the towers are only remotely concerned with trade, and if the towers had not been in existence the users of the office space would have had to locate elsewhere in properties that are not tax exempt, but are currently vacant.

In addition to the problems of coordination and economic inefficiency engendered by fragmentation, there is also a low level of public control and awareness of the activities of local government. This is well evidenced by the low voter turnout in many local government elections, and the number of positions filled by appointments on many boards of special districts. The result is that the vast bulk of the community is not represented. It is, therefore, not at all surprising to find that the property industry (real estate, builders, lawyers, insurance agents, etc.) and the financial institutions are heavily represented both in elected and appointed positions in the various levels of local government.

The issues facing the management of the major urban regions are, therefore, quite formidable for they involve a financial and governmental system that has developed and increased in complexity over many decades. The issues have to be resolved in the context of the types of services required and the geographic scale at which the function should be provided. The large *number* of local government units is not intrinsically bad, for the problems arise over the confusion and insularity of what they do, not the numbers themselves. Ideally, small jurisdictions should do what they do best and large jurisdictions should deal with those urban functions that they do best. The questions that arise, therefore, concern the size of unit that can perform different urban functions the best, and the most equitable method of financing these activities. Some approaches to the resolution of these issues that have been implanted in North America will be discussed in the next chapter.

ISSUES CONCERNING THE URBAN CONSUMPTION OF RURAL LAND

The general spreading of urban population, that is represented in a general way in the change exhibited between Figures 1.7 and 1.8, has an important impact on the present and future consumption of rural land for urban purposes. One of the problems in studying the impact of urban growth on the consumption of land is that data indicative of the trends is difficult to obtain. Ideally, land consumption rates, or the amount of land consumed per person for urban purposes, are determined from measures of the exact physical extent of the land used for urban purposes and the number of people residing on that land. To be able to examine change in land consumption rates, it would be necessary to know the way in which the occupancy of land for urban purposes has changed over time, as well as the numbers of people residing on that changing quantity of urban land. This type of information is virtually impossible to collect for the major urban regions as a whole because the actual limits of an urban area rarely match the statistical definitions used for census purposes. It is, however, possible to obtain estimates which can be used to give some idea as to the trends and severity of the issue in different areas.

The Urbanization of Rural Land Issue in the U.S.

Probably some of the best estimates of the amount of land consumed for urban purposes in the U.S. can be obtained from work undertaken by Otte[20] and Hart.[21] Both use data pertaining to "urbanized areas," which are central cities of 50,000 or more people plus the surrounding settled incorporated and unincorporated urban areas. These census units consist almost entirely of the closely built-up parts of the metropolis and are allowed to increase in geographical extent at the time of each decennial census to allow for the growth of the city. The urbanized area data reveal a steady increase in land consumption rates between 1950 and 1970. Using just the 157 "urbanized areas" in 1970 that were also "urbanized areas" in 1950, land consumption rates have increased from 0.184 acres per person in 1950 to 0.250 in 1960 and 0.283 in 1970. Although the magnitude of the land consumption rates appear to have been increasing at a decreasing rate over the time period, the implications are that new land is being consumed at extremely low densities.

There is, however, a considerable variation in urban land consumption rates among the major urban regions. In a detailed study of rural-urban land conversion in 53 fast-growth counties, using air photos, Zeimetz et al.[22] note that the average land consumption rates in these fast growth areas (0.173) was much less than the national average. Furthermore, the rates varied considerably between the major urban regions. In California (Santa Cruz and Santa Clara counties) the rate was 0.097 acres per person, on the Gulf Coast (Harris County-Houston) it was 0.202, in the high-growth counties of the Bosnywash areas about 0.160, in the lower Great Lakes area also about 0.160, and in Florida (along the Gulf Coast between Orlando-St. Petersburg and Ft. Myers) the rate reached a high of 0.481. These variations from region to region indicate that there are varying levels of control, chiefly exerted by price and secondarily by zoning regulations, which influence the rural-urban land consumption rate.

The intriguing aspect of these quite large land consumption rates in the major urban regions of the U.S. is that the urbanization of rural land is not considered to be an important issue. "Irrigation, drainage, and clearing add three times as much land annually to the cropland base as urbanization absorbs."[23] Thus, the general view is that "At the national level, urbanization has not greatly encroached upon the total supply of U.S. land used for crops."[24] There are concerns expressed amongst agriculturalists in Florida and California, but the public interest is involved with general environmental protection, not the preservation of agricultural lands. This lack of concern can, perhaps, be explained by the tremendous increases in farm productivity that have occurred since the 1950s as a result of the greater use of chemical fertilizers, new hybrids, and the introduction of different feed techniques.

Urbanization of Rural Land Issue in Canada

The most comprehensive set of data pertaining to the consumption of rural land for urban purposes in Canada has been assembled by Gierman.[25] The information for Canada as a whole indicates that land consumption rates have been increasing at a rate similar to that in the U.S., but that the general density of urban developments is somewhat greater than that in the U.S. As a consequence, land consumption rates are, on the average, lower than those in the U.S. For example, in the Windsor-Quebec City major urban region, the land consumption rate in 1961 is estimated to have been 0.130 acres per urban person, and 0.139 in 1971.[26] As these estimates involve more than half of the urban population in Canada, it is evident that the rates compare quite favorably with those for the U.S. as a whole.

Although the amount of land consumed per person for urban uses in Canada appears to be less than that in the U.S., and the rate of increase in land consumption rates between 1960 and 1970 also appears to be lower as well, the rural-urban land conversion issue is a matter of greater public concern in Canada than the U.S. The basic reason for this is that whereas in the U.S. there are about 340 million acres of good farm land, in Canada there are only about 55 million acres and of this less than 12 million acres is prime land in a reasonably good climatic situation. Urban areas in Canada are in direct competition for this prime land, and Gierman[27] demonstrates that over 60% of the land lost to urban uses between 1966 and 1971 was in the prime category. These losses have been particularly severe on the excellent tender fruit and truck farming lands in the Niagara Peninsula (Ont.) and the lower Fraser Valley of British Columbia (Vancouver). As a consequence, the loss of prime lands has become a public issue in Canada of equal importance to that of general environmental protection.

There are, therefore, a number of general issues facing the major urban regions of North America. Most of these issues are of concern to all of the regions, and they involve public policy decisions involving political processes. For these political processes to work, active interest, and occasionally public pressure, is required. The public cannot get involved unless there is an understanding of the nature of the causes of the issues, and possible public policy responses. In this and the previous chapter, there has been an attempt to outline the possible causes of differential growth, and the nature of some of the issues facing the major urban regions. The next chapter will be concerned with a discussion of the possible public policy responses to these issues and, where possible, the experience of the two political entities that exist on the North American continent will be compared. This comparison will demonstrate that even when two economic systems are essentially the same, slight differences in political structure permit different responses to the issues.

NOTES

[1] M. Yeates, "The Need for Environmental Perspectives on Issues Facing Older People" in S. Golant (ed.), *Location and Environment of Elderly Population* (Washington, D.C.: V. H. Winston & Sons, 1979).

[2] W. Alonso, "Metropolis Without Growth," *The Public Interest*, Vol. 4 (1978), pp. 68–86; and L. O. Stone and C. Marceau, *Canadian Population Trends and Public Policy Through the 1980s* (Montreal: McGill-Queen's University Press and I.R.P.P., 1977).

[3] P. A. Morrison, "Emerging Public Concerns over U.S. Population Movements in an Era of Slowing Growth" (Santa Monica, Calif.: The Rand Corporation, 1977), p. 5873.

[4] L. S. Bourne, "Some Myths of Canadian Urbanization: Reflections on the 1976 Census and Beyond," *Urbanism Past and Present*, Vol. 5 (1977–78), pp. 1–11.

[5] Ibid.

[6] M. Yeates, *Main Street: Windsor to Quebec City* (Toronto: Macmillan of Canada, 1975).

[7] J. W. Simmons, "Migration and the Canadian Urban System: Part II, Simple Relationships" (Toronto: Centre for Urban and Community Studies, University of Toronto, Research Paper No. 98).

[8] W. P. Beaton and J. L. Cox, "Toward an Accidental Urbanization Policy," *Journal of the American Institute of Planners* (Jan., 1977), pp. 54–61.

[9] A. R. Markusen and J. Fastrup, "The Regional War for Federal Aid," *The Public Interest*, Vol. 4 (1978), pp. 87–99.

[10] J. Mercer and J. Hultquist, "National Progress Toward Housing and Urban Renewal Goals" in J. S. Adams (ed.), *Urban Policymaking and Metropolitan Dynamics* (Cambridge, Mass.: Ballinger, 1976); and D. G. Bettison, *The Politics of Canadian Urban Development* (Edmonton: University of Alberta Press, 1975).

[11] D. M. Ray (ed.), *Canadian Urban Trends: Metropolitan Perspectives, Vol. II* (Toronto: Copp-Clark, 1976).

[12] W. P. Beaton and J. L. Cox, op. cit.

[13] A. R. Markusen and J. Fastrup, op. cit.

[14] Ibid., p. 96.

[15] H. W. Hallman, *Small and Large Together: Governing the Metropolis* (Beverly Hills: Sage Publications, 1977).

[16] Advisory Commission on Intergovernmental Relations, *Trends in Metropolitan America* (Washington, D.C.: GPO, 1977).

[17] Ibid., p. 8.

[18] W. K. Tabb, "The New York City Fiscal Crisis" in W. K. Tabb and L. Sawers (eds.), *Marxism and the Metropolis* (New York: Oxford University Press, 1978), pp. 243–245.

[19] Ibid., p. 256.

[20] R. C. Otte, *Farming in the City's Shadow, Urbanization of Land and Changes in Farm Output in Standard Metropolitan Statistical Areas, 1960-70* (Washington, D.C.: U.S. Department of Agriculture, ERS Report No. 250, 1974).

[21] J. F. Hart, "Urban Encroachment on Rural Areas," *Geographical Review*, Vol. 66 (1976), pp. 1-17.

[22] K. A. Zeimetz et al., *Dynamics of Land Use in Fast Growth Areas* (Washington, D.C.: USDA, A.E. Report 325, 1976).

[23] R. C. Otte, op. cit.

[24] K. A. Zeimetz et al., op. cit.

[25] D. Gierman, *Rural to Urban Land Conversion* (Ottawa: Lands Directorate, Fisheries and Environment, 1977).

[26] M. Yeates, op. cit., (1975).

[27] D. Gierman, op. cit.

Chapter 5

Some responses to the issues facing the major urban regions

In the previous chapter, some of the issues facing the major urban regions have been defined as concerning demographic conditions, the location of economic activities, urban goverment and finances, and the consumption of rural land for urban purposes. In particular, the demographic issues involve economic and political factors influencing migration and immigration; the issues of urban government concern fragmentation and the revenue-expenditures gap; and the land issue involves increasing land consumption rates and the removal of prime lands from agricultural production. Although these issues face each of the urban regions, they vary in importance and the land issue is more of a matter of public concern in Canada than the U.S.

In this chapter, these issues will be examined further, particularly with respect to some of the different public policy responses that have been implemented, or may be proposed, to alleviate the problems that result. Although the public policy implications of the various theories that have been proposed as explanations for differential growth have been outlined in Chapter 3, and also some public policy consequences of the issues discussed in Chapter 4 have been mentioned previously, the purpose of this section is to draw these various threads together. Furthermore, some of the differences in approaches to these public policy questions between the U.S. and Canada may generate alternative perspectives, for urban planning can gain from an understanding of the experiences of the two countries. If, at times, the discussion seems to be overly "Canadian," this is only to redress the imbalance noted by Corbett,[1] which is that Americans, in general, know little about the Canadian urban experience.

RESPONSES TO DEMOGRAPHIC ISSUES

The major demographic assumption with respect to population growth in North America over the next few decades is that the fertility rate will continue to be only a little above the replacement level, and that the increase in population that does occur will be mostly as a result of decreases in the death rate, increases in the length of life, and immigration. The consequence of this assumption is that internal migration and the destination of immigrants will play increasingly important roles in differential urban growth. The influence of migration, under conditions of low rates of natural increase, on differential urban growth are illustrated in Table 5.1. This table presents those large metropolitan areas (population greater than 500,000) in the major urban regions which experienced decreases in population between 1970 and 1975. The natural increase and net migration components of the decrease in population for 1970 and 1975 are compared with the same components of change for 1960 and 1970. Whereas only 2 of the large metropolises (Jersey City and Pittsburgh) experienced declines in SMSA population in the 1960/1970 period, 12 experienced declines in the 1970/75 period. The combination of decreases in the rate of natural increase, which in most cases declined by about 40% between the two periods, and negative increments in net migration are quite dramatic.

Internal Migration

Net migration, it must be recalled, is the sum of migrants into the area less the number of migrants who left the area. Frequently the volumes of in-migration and out-migration for a metropolitan area are quite large, and even though the net migration statistic may be small, the change in characteristics of the population resulting could be quite significant. For example, if most of the out-migrants were in the 20–30 year age group and with a reasonable level of education, and most of the in-migrants were less well educated and in older age groups with a number of young dependents, the socio-economic characteristics of the urban region could change quite considerably even though the net migration statistic might be quite small. This is, in fact, the type of situation that has occurred in a number of declining urban regions, for a high proportion of the volume of out-migrants involves the younger and better educated component of the labor force. The result is that there are more persons of working age in the metropolises of net positive migration, and relatively fewer persons of working age in the metropolises of net negative migration. Concomitantly, there are relatively more dependents per capita in the declining metropolises, and fewer dependents per capita in the growing metropolises.

Another aspect of the net-migration statistics, as presented for declining metropolises in Table 5.1, concerns the destination of the migrants from the major metropolises. Ten of the 12 declining metropolises are located in major urban regions that exhibited quite low population growth rates between 1970 and 1975, whereas two (Los Angeles and Seattle) are in areas that exhibited above average rates of growth. The out-migration from these two areas may, therefore, be

Table 5.1. Components of population decrease for the large metropolitan areas in the major urban regions, 1970/75.

SMSA	Annual rate, 1960/1970			Annual rate, 1970/1975		
	Natural increase	Net migration	Population change	Natural increase	Net migration	Population change
New York	0.8	-0.1	0.8	0.4	-1.1	-0.7
Philadelphia	0.9	0.0	1.0	0.5	-0.6	-0.1
Newark	0.9	0.0	0.9	0.5	1.1	0.6
Providence, etc.	0.7	-0.0	0.7	0.4	-0.5	-0.1
Jersey City	0.7	-0.8	-0.1	0.4	-1.2	-0.8
Pittsburgh	0.7	-0.7	-0.0	0.2	-0.9	-0.7
Cleveland	1.0	-0.2	0.8	0.6	-1.4	-0.8
Buffalo	0.9	-0.6	0.3	0.4	-0.7	0.3
Los Angeles–Long Beach	1.2	0.4	1.5	0.7	-1.0	-0.3
Cincinnati	1.1	-0.3	0.9	0.7	-0.7	-0.0
Dayton	1.3	0.3	1.6	0.9	-1.2	-0.3
Seattle–Everett	1.1	1.5	2.5	0.5	-0.7	-0.2

Source: U.S. Bureau of the Census, *Current Population Reports*, Series P-25, No. 709, Washington, D.C.: U.S. Department of Commerce.

absorbed by the faster growing metropolises within the same region, whereas the out-migration from the other urban areas is probably leaving the urban region altogether, as is demonstrated by Figure 4.1. A more detailed example of this particular point can be gained from the different growth experiences of the areas surrounding the metropolises of Montreal and Toronto within the Windsor-Quebec City major urban region.

Migration data for these two metropolises is included in Table 5.2. As the information contained within this table is rather more detailed than that in Table 5.1, an explanatory note is probably in order. First, migration is partitioned into net migrants from within Canada, and net immigration to the metropolises from outside the country, for the 1966/1971 period. This type of partition is not presented in Table 5.1, where the net migration rates involve both internal and external migration. Thus, the net migration rates for some metropolises, such as New York City and Los Angeles, may be quite wrong because, as has been observed previously, immigration into the U.S. in recent years is an unknown statistic. While the Canadian data is by no means perfect, the immigration information is considerably more accurate. The fertility rates refer to the number of children born per woman who has ever been married, and the 1971 statistic is obviously inflated by the high birthrates of the 1950s and 1960s. Nevertheless, it is noticeable that there is a considerable difference among the larger metropolises in the fertility rate, with Toronto having a rate only slightly above the replacement level, and Quebec City having the highest. Since 1971, there has been a considerable decline in the fertility rate in the Province of Quebec, to a level below that in the Province of Ontario and less than the national average.

It is noticeable from Table 5.2 that both Montreal and Toronto experienced a loss of population of similar magnitudes as a result of internal migration. This loss is, however, based on a large volume of in-migration from, and out-migration

Table 5.2. Components of population change in the larger metropolitan areas of the Windsor–Quebec City major urban region, and Vancouver, 1966/1971.

Component of change	CMA					
	Montreal	Toronto	Ottawa–Hull	Quebec City	Hamilton	Vancouver
1971 population (thousands)	2,731	2,602	620	501	503	1,082
Fertility rate	2.45	2.13	2.55	2.85	2.33	2.20
In-migrants, 1966/1971	277,300	346,900	124,500	83,900	81,100	267,200
Out-migrants, 1966/1971	307,600	391,800	98,200	64,200	94,100	190,200
Net migrants	−30,300	−44,900	26,300	19,700	−13,000	76,000
Net immigrants	88,100	250,500	17,900	3,200	20,900	56,900

Sources: Department of Manpower and Immigration (1975), *Internal Migration and Immigrant Settlement*, Ottawa: Information Canada; Statistics Canada, *Fertility in Canada*, 99-706; Bulletin 5.1-6.

to, the rest of Canada. The important questions, therefore, relate to (1) the source and socio-economic characteristics of the in-migrants, and (2) the destination and socio-economic characteristics of the out-migrants. The major source of in-migrants to Montreal is the combined region east of Ontario, mainly rural Quebec, and consists of people in the younger age groups with limited education. The major source of in-migrants to Toronto are better educated "anglos" from Montreal and single people from the Maritimes. The prime destination of out-migrants from Montreal is to areas west of the Province of Quebec, primarily Toronto and Vancouver. But, the prime destination of out-migrants from Toronto is the urban communities of southeastern Ontario surrounding the metropolis, and most of the movers involve middle-income families. Thus, whereas the negative net migration with respect to Montreal signifies a real loss of productive labor from southern Quebec, the negative net migration with respect to Toronto represents part of the decentralization of productive capacity and population from Toronto to its surrounding tributary region.

Internal migration patterns create issues of public policy concern, therefore, when they stimulate or reinforce economic divergence. This economic divergence is usually exemplified by higher unemployment, lower per capita incomes, and higher levels of out-migration in the declining areas. These symptoms become issues of concern when they exist for a fairly lengthy period of time, or involve large enough numbers of people, such that the situation cannot be ignored politically. If the out-migration is of the type represented by Montreal, then the responses have to be geared toward macro-regional readjustment. If, on the other hand, the out-migration is of the type represented by Toronto, then the concerns involve inequalities resulting from decentralization within a spreading urban region.

Macro-regional Responses. As has been indicated in Chapter 3, the response to macro-regional shifts in economic opportunities depends quite clearly on the explanation that appears most acceptable for the differential growth patterns. Although the various situations in North America can be "explained" in terms of economic convergence, the staples model, economic divergence, and economic control, the response is invariably formulated within the context of one of these, and the explanation chosen usually reflects the political ideology of the person or group responsible for formulating the response. Some examples may illustrate this contention that the response is derivative of the explanation that is accepted.

Proponents of the economic convergence explanation generally argue either that the rapidly growing areas are becoming more like the declining areas with the passage of time, or that studies demonstrating continuing divergence in growth despite convergence in some important indicators are based on a misinterpretation of the convergence measures used. The former argument is predicated upon the assumption that business activities have, for example, located in metropolitan and nonmetropolitan areas in the south and west because of lower levels of local taxation and lower costs of living which permit the payment of lower wage costs. The lower costs of local taxation arise due to the fact that the urban areas are newer, so that the infrastructure works more efficiently and has yet to incur repair and replacement costs, and that the local governments provide a lower level of physical and social services, such as public transport.[2] However, with the passage of time, the infrastructure of these newer cities becomes older and has to be repaired or replaced, and as more people move into the urban region, more physical and social services are demanded by the electorate. Hence, these newer cities of the south and west will begin to exhibit the same diseconomies of urban agglomeration as those in the northeast, and, as a consequence, economic activities will cease to be attracted to the area.

Although information such as that presented in Table 3.1 demonstrates a convergence of certain measures of regional differences, the urban regions of the south and west continue to grow faster than those of the north and east. This continued greater growth is invariably explained in terms of regional differences in industry mix, labor productivity, cost of living indices, age of capital stock, extent of unionization, etc. One feature of these measures that is invariably ignored is the propensity for manufacturing firms to locate in smaller southern towns, where the wage rates that are paid tend to be lower.[3] Thus, although general measures may demonstrate developing convergence, the basic difference between the size of places in which firms locate in the north and south, and the effect that this has on labor costs, still persist. It is argued, of course, that in time these small town-large city differentials will narrow, and eventually cease to be a factor in the location decision of the manufacturers, and, at that time, the migration balance which currently favors the south will no longer be as evident.

In some cases, the staples approach may provide a tenable explanation for growth or decline in a major urban region, and the response depends upon the economic state of the basic activity. If the basic activity was a natural resource that has now become exhausted or no longer in demand, then the response can only be to find another set of activities for the region, or allow the region to stagnate and the more mobile portion of the population to leave. Government incentives may be used to encourage the location of new activities in the area, and the type of incentives that are used should be related to the nature of the manufacturing activity that the region wishes to attract and the socio-economic structure of the region to receive the incentive.[4] If, for example, the policy is to renovate the existing industry and make it more efficient to compete with others, then incentives involving tax holidays for capital investments, and capital grants, may be considered appropriate. New economic activities to make use of local labor may be attracted by per capita grants for each new job created, and the construction of new buildings with associated infrastructure for new plants. While programs of this kind may be successful in some areas, such as Scranton–Wilkes Barre, where a number of new activities have replaced many based on coal mining, the subsidy approach often results in the luring of an activity which departs from the area once the period of the bribe expires.

The economic divergence model has particularly important implications as far as redevelopment is concerned. These implications are particularly relevant with respect to areas that may have per capita incomes equal to, or greater than, the national average, but are experiencing limited growth as a result of a poor industry-mix. In these situations, the multiplier effect is extremely important because limiting the negative multiplier impact in times of stagnation, and reinforcing the multiplier effect in times of economic stimulation, can greatly influence the state of the local economy and thus influence the volume of migration. In the case of urban areas that have a poor industry-mix, such as in many metropolitan regions in the lower Great Lakes and Bosnywash major urban regions, the task is to prevent continuing stagnation and declining income levels by encouraging the introduction of economic activities that can take advantage of the agglomeration economies that exist. This implies the careful selection and encouragement of activities that can generate forward and backward linkages with other firms in the local economy, and at the same time introduce firms having a higher rate of growth into the industry-mix. This may well require the joint persuasion of local, state or provincial, and federal government authorities. In order to achieve maximum and long-term benefits, the new activities that are introduced must generate a pattern of circular and cumulative growth through interlinkages with as many other elements of the urban economy as possible.

The economic control perspective focusses attention quite specifically on the individuals, corporations, and governments who direct economic activities to specific areas, and away from others, and hence influence migration streams. Angel,[5] for example, suggests that the energy and political savvy of local entrepreneurs in Houston permitted that city to grow rather than Galveston, even though it lay 60 miles inland with far inferior port facilities. The construction of the Houston ship channel allowed the city to syphon off trade from the coastal port, and placed in a better position to take advantage of later developments in the petrochemical industry and space technology. The evidence with respect to the location of corporations and decision-making responsibilities does, however, reveal the difference between the spread of employment generating activities and the control of these activities. While growth has continued apace in the south and west, and many subsidiaries have been established in these areas, most of the headquarter offices remain in New York City and Chicago.

Whereas New York City was the location of the headquarter offices of 31% of the largest 500 U.S. manufacturing organizations in 1960, it remained the location of 29% in 1972.[6] As a whole, the metropolises of the Bosnywash and lower Great Lakes urban regions were the location of the headquarter offices of 65% of the largest 500 U.S. manufacturing corporations in 1960, and slightly more than 60% in 1972. Thus, though there has been a decline in economic control, the older cities of the north and east still contain the decision-making components of the largest corporations. Similarly, Toronto had become the location of the headquarter offices of 33% of the largest Canadian companies by 1974,[7] and Montreal and Toronto together are the location of more than 51% of the headquarter offices of the largest companies. Trends in the mid 1970s would suggest that the concentration of control in and around Toronto has increased at the expense of Montreal. Thus, though there has been a shift of productive activity and population from the Bosnywash and lower Great Lakes urban regions, the economic power still lies in these regions.[8] Thus, the Sunbelt area, and Canada beyond the Windsor–Quebec City axis, may be regarded as regions that are still controlled economically (and politically) by the historic heartland along the east coast and around the lower Great Lakes.

Under these circumstances, the response has to focus on the apparent contradiction between the regional shift in the location of much of the productive capacity of corporations, as compared with the continued concentration of decision-making in the heartland areas. Proponents of the economic control perspective[9] argue that this is a logical outcome of capitalist development. Whereas capitalist organizations can reinforce their power by concentrating their decision-making activities and developing strong linkages (via interlinked boards of directors) with each other and the political decision-making structure (in Washington, D.C.), control over labor can be best maintained by diffusing the productive capacity in plants around the continent, and particularly in those places where collective activities (such as those through unions) are not held in high esteem, and year-round recreational activities provide an outlet for worker frustration. Thus, the changes that have occurred among the major urban regions of North America merely reflect the continued effort by capitalists for the maximization of both quantitative and qualitative efficiency.

If it is considered that the regional shift in jobs[10] and the resulting stagnation of certain areas are counter to the national interest, then the economic control interpretation leads fairly automatically to a demand for some level of influence by the state in the decisions of the corporations. This may be achieved both directly and indirectly. Direct influence can be exerted through the nationalization of the key large corporations, or through a requirement for much greater public input into the decision-making processes of these corporations. Indirect intervention can take the form of the use of government purchasing, the location of civilian employment and defense facilities, and the granting of contracts, to counter the actions of private industry. Responses of the latter kind are probably easier to implement in North American society than those involving direct intervention, even though the web of linkages between government and the large corporations is now so complex that this form of influence would be difficult.

Micro-regional Responses. The chief issue of a micro-regional nature, which has been discussed in the previous chapter, concerns the inner city/outer city disparity question. To this must be added the type of situation exemplified by the internal migration statistics for Montreal, which involves migration from the metropolitan area to other regions beyond the province. Regions such as these, and particularly the inner cities, involve areas that consist of a population that is, on the average, relatively poor (though there are pockets of extreme wealth in nearly every inner city) and exhibit an absolute decline in economic activities and employment. In these cases, the task is to foster redevelopment, which does not imply a necessity for growth, and also redirect local labor resources to opportunities for employment. The responses to these situations can be most productively discussed in terms of economic divergence and economic control, for convergence is unlikely in these areas and the staple approach is too simple or inappropriate an explanation.

In terms of the economic divergence model, the structure of decline as exemplified by the cumulative causation framework in Figure 3.3 provides some useful indications of the type of responses that are required. The responses should be directed towards (1) limiting the loss of local job opportunities, (2) limiting the disintegration of localization economies, and (3) preventing the deterioration of local service infrastructure. Programs directed toward limiting the loss of local job opportunities involve some measures to prevent economic activities that might leave, such as favorable insurance and tax rates. Other programs could, through labor subsidies, help to promote the creation of new jobs. The important elements of the local economic structure that generate localization economies need to be identified, and these supported in a similar manner. Finally, the local physical (transport facilities and serviced industrial buildings and land) and service (schools, health care facilities) infrastructure must be maintained through such measures as higher per capita federal and state or provincial grants to declining areas.

The economic control perspective suggests, however, that redevelopment in a number of urban regions requires more than the responses generated through the explanation offered by the economic divergence model. The migration of productive capital from these areas, being the consequence of a desire for quantitative and qualitative efficiency, can only be countered by forms of direct and/or indirect intervention by the state, as outlined in the preceding section. For example, with respect to the inner city, this perspective suggests that redevelopment requires the establishment of a public agency that is given the specific task, and necessary level of funding, to renovate housing, change land uses where needed, revitalize local physical and service infrastructure, and generate employment opportunities for the inhabitants of the area. In this context, one interpretation of the independence movement in Quebec concerns the desire for control, by the Quebecois, of the economic activities in the province in order to foster development on the basis of local resources.

Factionalism. In the absence of public policy responses to some of the issues arising from internal migration, the result has been the exacerbation of factionalism. Although, on a countrywide basis, it does not matter whether a well-trained accountant moves from Philadelphia to Pensacola, or London (Ontario) to Vancouver, for the costs of the training have been incurred within the nation, on a local basis the migration is quite significant. This is because educational costs are borne locally, so Philadelphia and Pennsylvania have lost the accumulated investment in the accountant, and Pensacola and Florida have gained an accountant for nothing. Though this might not be terribly significant during times of fairly equal regional growth, during periods of considerable differences in migration flows such imbalances can create tensions between states, provinces, and regions.

Issues arising from these types of selective migration patterns have, of course, begun to reach crisis proportions in many inner cities and metropolitan areas, particularly but not only located within the Bosnywash and lower Great Lakes urban regions. Migration patterns have resulted in central cities containing a disproportionate number of elderly, poor, and ill-trained. The north and east may also have borne a disproportionate share of the educational costs of the U.S., and Ontario may be in the process of incurring a similar situation with respect to the Canadian west. Inequities of this kind are generating factionalism, as is evidenced by the demands of many northern and eastern central city mayors for a higher per capita weighting on revenue sharing for inner city populations, which are countered by some Sunbelt mayors with demands for special federal subsidies to cater for rapid growth.

On a regional basis, the bias in areas of growth and decline could well lead to political schisms of some consequence.[11] Political power is based on economic strength and number of votes, and the areas in which decline is occurring are beginning to witness some disappearance of this power. Hence the formation of the Coalition of Northeast Governors, the Northeast-Midwest Economic Advancement Coalition, the Southern Growth Policies Board, and the Parti Québecois. East-West political rivalries are becoming even more accentuated in the U.S., and Ontario-Quebec-Alberta-British Columbia insularities more evident in Canada. These developing factionalisms can only serve to exacerbate a situation in which probably the best solution is to recognize that these are national problems, and that such problems are the responsibility of the nation as a whole. The national concern would, with this response, involve such matters as health, welfare, housing for low income families and the older population, and education. This is, of course, a contentious response to the issues arising from internal migration, and factionalism only serves to make the response more contentious.

Immigration

The effect of immigration on differential urban growth can be extremely important. Although the census information for urban areas in the U.S. undoubtedly severely understates the amount of immigration in many large southwestern metropolises and New York City, the information for Canadian metropolitan areas indicates just how important this component can be. The information in Table 5.2 indicates quite clearly that without immigration, the populations of Toronto, Montreal, and Hamilton would have incurred population increases as a result of migration. In the Toronto case, for example, internal migration yielded in the 1966/71 period a net loss of nearly 45,000 people, but with net immigration yielding 250,000 new inhabitants to the area, migration as a whole resulted in a population increase of a little more than 205,000 for the 5-year period. The variation of the destination of immigrants among the major Canadian urban regions is indicated in Table 5.3, where for the 1961/1971 period immigration accounted for more than three-quarters of the population increase in Toronto, 26% in Montreal, and only 4% in Quebec City.

The impact of immigration on urban growth in the 1970s and 1980s becomes even more apparent when it is realized that quite high percentages for many of the metropolises in Table 5.3 occurred during a period of substantial, but diminishing, rates of natural increase. If it is assumed that the legal plus illegal immigration into the U.S. is now similar in comparative volume (per capita) as that into Canada during the 1960s, then about 50% of the population increase in the 1970s in a number of metropolitan areas in the California and Gulf Coast urban regions must be attributable to this particular source. The responses to issues arising from relatively large volumes of immigration of this kind vary throughout the continent.

The Canadian response is to try to relate the volume of immigration to national manpower needs, and the language requirements of the Province of Quebec. One fear in Quebec was that a large volume of non-French speaking immigrants would

Table 5.3. Number of foreign born living in CMA who immigrated in the period 1961/1971 as a percent of the metropolitan area increase between 1961 and 1971, Canadian urban regions.

CMA	Percent foreign born
Montreal	26
Toronto	76
Ottawa–Hull	16
Quebec	4
Hamilton	38
Kitchener	28
London	18
Windsor	21
Vancouver	30
Victoria	21

Source: Department of Manpower and Immigration (1975), *Internal Migration and Immigrant Settlement*, Ottawa: Information Canada.

strain the cultural homogeneity of that province, hence the linguistic requirements of Bill 101. The Quebec government has now negotiated an agreement with the federal government that gives the province a greater degree of control in this area. The U.S. has long tried to influence the mix of immigrants through various quota systems, but with illegal immigration probably doubling the legal volume, it is apparent that the immigration policy is not well articulated. The result is the creation of an "underclass" of workers who have no rights, and, who, from an economic control perspective, inhibit the collective power of some groups of labor (such as farm workers and hotel service employment) with whom they compete. The response to this illegal immigration, apart from a few border incidents, has been minimal, perhaps because there are too many interest groups who see value in the creation of an "underclass" of this kind.

The urban impact of this immigration has, however, been quite important, and is often ignored. To return to the Canadian situation, one aspect of Canadian cities, particularly Toronto, that has attracted attention from the U.S. is the comparative health of Canadian central cities vis-à-vis those in the U.S. While there are many reasons for this, such as the later development of post-World War II suburbanization and the implementation of metropolitan government, there is no doubt that immigration has played a key role. During the 1950s and 1960s, the internal migration of the black population toward the central cities in the U.S. served to replace the white middle classes who were vacating the inner city for the suburbs. During the 1960s, the immigration of Italians, Portuguese, etc. to Canadian central cities served to replace the middle-class population that was migrating to the suburbs and smaller southern Ontario cities. When the in-flow of the black population to the U.S. inner cities began to slow down in the late 1960s and virtually cease in the 1970s, then the population of the central cities and eventually the metropolitan areas of which they are a part began to decline. By contrast, immigration into Canada has maintained a level of population in-flow into the larger central cities.

The implication of the observations is that responses to national concerns with respect to the volume, type, language requirements, etc., of immigrants can have severe consequences on central cities and metropolitan development. In particular, the comparative health of Canadian inner cities is probably related directly to the volume of external immigration, and the price of reducing the volume of immigration may be the creation of a declining central city economic base, abandonment, and the loss of vitality that has become endemic to many cities in the U.S. Extending this discussion to Montreal, it is quite apparent that immigration (of chiefly Italians) during the 1960s accounted for a reasonable proportion of its growth. Strict language requirements will, undoubtedly, reduce the in-flow of immigrants, and this, combined with a decline in the fertility rate to almost the ZPG level and a continuation of the negative net internal migration situation, could well result in an actual decline in the population of that metropolis in the near future.

There are, as a consequence, quite severe and often dramatic effects on urban areas from responses, whether they be from governments, business, or the public, to demographic issues. Furthermore, many questions of a demographic nature are quite difficult to predict, so the urban impacts become equally as difficult to estimate. The change in the rate of natural population increase has resulted in an enormous array of issues, ranging from economic to public finance, facing urban areas, and the volitility of the fertility rate during the past two decades leaves no assurance that present trends may continue indefinitely. There are, however, no other bases than present trends for making short-term predictions, but the responses must be cautious and carefully articulated.

RESPONSES WITH RESPECT TO METROPOLITAN FINANCE AND ORGANIZATION

The nature of the financial and organizational problems facing large major urban regions has been discussed in the previous chapter. The responses to these issues are quite diverse, one of the most dramatic being the "taxpayer" revolt crystallized in Proposition 13 in California and the many similar efforts to reduce the burden of the property, and other local taxes, elsewhere in North America. At the outset, it should be recognized that the possible array of responses to these issues varies quite considerably between Canada and the U.S. as a result of the different constitutional arrangements in each of the federations. Under the British North

America Act of 1867, which defines the structure of Canadian federalism, the provincial governments have quite explicit powers, while the central government (the Parliament in Ottawa) has powers relating to the common interests of the nation as a whole, and residual powers not explicitly granted to the provinces. In the U.S., the federal government has quite explicit powers as stated in the Constitution (1787) and its subsequent Amendments, while the states have general and residual powers relating to their particular geographical jurisdictions. These differences have important repercussions with respect to local government.

At the time of the preparation of the BNA Act, and the Constitution of the U.S., both countries were essentially agrarian in economic structure. Of course, by 1867 the U.S. had developed quite large urban areas, but Canadian cities at that time were, by comparison, small and depended directly on trade and service activities with their hinterlands. As a consequence, municipal structure, finance, and organization were not considered matters of tremendous importance at the time of the preparation of the two constitutions. In Canada, the BNA Act states quite explicitly that provincial legislatures have sovereignty over municipal institutions, which includes the power to establish the structure and geographical jurisdiction of local governments, the array of responsibilities, and the ways in which they may receive and raise revenues. In the U.S., the Constitution does not mention governments below the state level, and, as a consequence, local governments have developed in response to local needs and aspirations, and the power of the local community is a great deal stronger in the U.S. than in Canada. One interesting result of this is that state constitutions are now filled with protective devices for local governments, and these consist primarily of protections against excessive interference by state governments into the affairs of local municipalities.

These constitutional differences are one of the major reasons why the reform of local government is far easier in Canada than the U.S.[12] Canadian provincial legislatures can implement new forms of local government through the actions of provincial parliaments, and, while they might not wish to antagonize too many voters in a local area, nevertheless the implementation of new structures does not depend on a majority vote and plebiscite within the area involved. In the U.S., such direct action for reform is far more difficult for state governments are reluctant to initiate changes involving local governments and will not act on any local initiatives unless they are sure of having the majority support of each of the different local areas affected by the proposed governmental restructuring. Thus, changes in the structure and finance of local government in response to the spread of population within the major urban regions, and the actual physical coalescence of many metropolises, are more possible in Canada than the U.S. because of the slightly different constitutional frameworks within which both countries operate.

The possibilities for local government reform are also enhanced by the attitudes of the Canadian population toward local government reform. Whereas the population of the U.S. is, in general, imbued with the notion of local autonomy and independence, which is exemplified politically by a desire for as much local control as possible, the Canadian population appears (on the whole) to have a more open attitude toward reform involving larger units of metropolitan government, and the transference of some social responsibilities (such as health and welfare) to the provincial and/or national governments. This difference in attitude may well be the result of the massive immigration from western Europe that occurred to Canada in the post-World War II period, for much of this population came from metropolitan areas and highly urbanized countries where social matters had been recognized as national responsibilities, as well as the responsibility of metropolitan-wide governments.

Although many responses to the fiscal and fragmentation issues have been suggested, they may be grouped into two categories. First, there are those that involve reforms within the framework of current political structures, and do not focus at all on the way in which decisions are made concerning urban capital investments as explained by the economic control argument. These reforms are labelled "structural," and will be discussed at some length for all the responses within North America have been within this framework, and the ones most likely to be implemented are also of this type. The second set of responses are more "radical" as they focus quite explicitly on the ownership of capital and the way in which capital investments are made within urban regions, and the benefits are appropriated.

Structural Responses to Fiscal Issues

Fiscal issues are primarily concerned with fiscal imbalance and the most equitable means for raising revenue. The responses to these issues invariably involve (1) the transfer of funds to local governments from higher levels of government, (2) the transfer of some responsibilities currently assumed by many municipalities to higher levels of government or the special bodies, and (3) the creation of new means of revenue-raising by local governments. Each of these involves a variety of measures and has different political implications, and there are many interpretations as to their past, and future likelihood, of success.

Financial Transfers. The increasing importance of financial transfers to local governments has been emphasized in the previous chapter in the discussion concerning Table 4.4. By 1975, financial transfers in the U.S. from state governments to local governments provided as much revenue as property taxes, and the relative contribution from this source to the budgets of municipalities had increased by almost 60% in a 10-year period. The relative contribution of "other" sources, which are mostly federal funds, increased by almost 125% in the same period.

Table 5.4 provides an example of the difference in sources of revenue received by, and the transfer of money between, the three different levels of government in the Windsor-Quebec City major urban region for 1970. The federal government received 58% of its revenue from personal and corporate taxes, and the rest from "other" sources, such as import duties, licensing fees, etc. The provincial governments of Ontario and Quebec received around 30% of their revenues from personal and corporate taxes, about 50% from "other" sources, and the remainder in the form of conditional or direct grants from the federal government. The local governments received most of their income from property taxes, some from "other" sources (such as sales taxes), and a large proportion in the form of conditional

Table 5.4. Comparison of the percentage distribution of the sources of revenue for the federal, provincial, and local government levels.

Level of government	Income tax[a]	Property tax	Transfer from provincial	Transfer from federal	Other
Federal	58.0	0.7			41.3
Provincial					
Ontario	27.2			16.8	56.0
Quebec	31.6			22.0	46.4
Local					
Ontario		44.0	39.2	1.8	19.0
Quebec		38.5	43.0	0.6	17.9

[a] Individual and corporation.
Source: Yeates (1975), p. 293.

transfers and grants from the provincial governments. There is, therefore, in the Canadian system a "trickle-down" process, with transfers from the federal to the provincial levels, and from the provincial to the local levels.

In the U.S., local governments receive financial transfers from both the federal and state levels of government, and the amount contributed by the property tax is, proportionately, a great deal less. The trend to decreasing reliance on the property tax will, in the future, result in much greater reliance being placed on federal and state transfers, and the implementation of revenue sharing in 1972 with the federal government has accelerated this trend. Unfortunately, the revenue-sharing disbursements have been on a per capita basis, which favors the faster growing suburban areas and cities in the south and western parts of the U.S. A new formula for revenue sharing is required which takes into account the particular needs of the central cities. There is, at the moment, limited recognition of the special requirement of these areas in the revenue-sharing formula, but this is not at a scale sufficient to take into account the enormous amount of social service and infrastructure support that is required.

Although financial transfers are the most likely response to the fiscal imbalance facing many local governments, they are not, in the long run, the real answer to the problem. In the first place, many of the grants are conditional, requiring matching expenditures in certain activities at the local level, or implementation of certain services. Many local governments feel that conditional grants impose activities which are not a high priority as far as they are concerned, and that this results in inefficient expenditure patterns. Conditional federal and state, or conditional provincial, transfers, may impose inappropriate national, state or provincial priorities on local communities. Secondly, urban areas require a fiscal base which is equitable and expands (or contracts) according to the socio-economic situation of the inhabitants of the area. The volume of conditional grants and revenue-sharing funds vary according to the political perception of the need, and in times of "belt-tightening" financial transfers to urban areas are the first to be cut. Thus, the politics of factionalism, discussed previously, is likely to result in decreasing revenues to those major urban regions, and those parts of metropolises, that are in the greatest need.

Transfer of Responsibilities. The second group of responses involves the transfer of certain responsibilities, now partially funded by taxes raised by local governments, to the state or provincial, and federal, levels of government. The basic premise for this response rests on the fact that there are a number of activities that are financed in whole or in part by local government which yield benefits, or serve, the state, province or nation as a whole, and are, therefore, really of concern to the higher level governments. This argument is particularly applicable to education, health, and other social services, for the benefits of good and sensitive programs in these areas are realized by areas well beyond the boundaries of particular local government units. Furthermore, the establishment of local areas of higher and lower quality creates inequalities of opportunity which perpetuate class differences.

The basic premise for the transfer of responsibilities response is reinforced by the proliferation and variety of responsibilities accepted by local governments. For example, New York City bears the costs of municipal hospitals, large public universities, and a large share of the welfare costs. Although other cities assume responsibilities of these kinds, they do not undertake all three. The city of Chicago, which is regarded as relatively solvent, is served by a hospital system which is financed by Cook County (currently in huge debt), post-secondary public education financed by the state of Illinois, and a welfare system funded largely by the state and federal governments. To give some idea of the effect of cost sharing involving transfers of money form the federal level to local governments, consider the case of Medicaid for the elderly in New York City. This vital service is received by about 10% of the city's population, and the cost of providing the service has risen 25% per annum between 1971 and 1976.[13] Under the cost-sharing agreements, New York City pays one-fourth of all Medicaid costs and is caught in a financial treadmill, for the city contains an increasingly disproportionate large share of the elderly population and medical costs have incurred the greatest increases due to inflation.

It is for this reason that many people[14] advocate the transfer of all welfare and health responsibilities to the federal government in the U.S. Wade, for example, notes that expenditures in these areas presently ". . . follow fifty different state patterns which were devised years before the present crisis which have not been substantially revised."[15] Furthermore, the major urban regions of Bosnywash, the lower Great Lakes, and the Ohio Valley, tend to have a larger share of the older population of the U.S. and also higher rates of unemployment, and, as a consequence, bear a larger burden of localized national welfare and health costs than the more rapidly growing urbanized parts of the nation. Of course, these costs are placing an impossible burden on the inner cities of these regions, for they have lost a considerable portion of their revenue-producing population and economic activities, and gained an increasing share of the population in need.

The federalization of welfare and health responsibilities in the U.S. involves a whole set of political issues which are far from being resolved. On the one hand, the American Medical Association views the federalization of health responsibilities as a major step towards the "socialization" of medicine and doctors, while this conservative view is opposed by more liberal groups who see federalization as a natural response to the problem of providing equal access to health care for the entire population. The fiscal dilemma facing Canadian municipalities is much less acute in this regard, for most provinces have already instituted provincial health care schemes, and welfare is also a matter of provincial and federal concern. This is, therefore, another reason for the greater comparative "health" of Canadian cities, for many responsibilities that are causing nightmares in U.S. cities have been accepted as the responsibilities of higher levels of government which have a financial base, and cost control mechanisms, that are more suited to the provision of these particular services.

New Methods of Revenue Raising. A third group of responses involves a variety of proposals that have been directed toward the raising of additional revenue for local government, and the creation of new sources of finance. The property tax is essentially regressive, that is, it creates a heavier proportional tax burden on lower income individual families than those in the higher income brackets, and it also fails to recoup to local government the values created as a result of public investments. This is because the property tax, as currently levied in most communities, is based primarily on the value of the improvements, i.e., the buildings on the land, and secondarily on an estimated value of the land. Carey[16] points out that a tax on improvements set at 3% of the market value of the property per year amounts to a lump sum sales tax on a 20-year investment of 52%.

Thus a property tax that is based primarily on improvements is a severe detriment to reinvestment, particularly in inner cities, for unimproved land incurs minimal taxation, while improved land is taxed quite highly. If the property tax were replaced by a land value tax, in which the land were taxed as high as possible while the value of the buildings were taxed at minimal amounts, then land would become expensive to hold and redevelopment, to gain income from the property to pay the tax on the land, would become a priority. If an owner did not want to redevelop the land, then the high taxes would encourage him to sell to someone who might. A land value tax would, therefore, promote redevelopment and at the same time provide a means for regaining values created as a result of adjacent public investments, such as highways or subway facilities.

Apart from reformulating the property tax, new methods of revenue raising could also be allocated to local governments. One such tax that has been suggested is a municipal income tax, of which the simplest is a fixed proportion of the total income received by the inhabitants of the community. The levy of a city income tax has to be approved by the local community, and in times of crisis (such as in Cleveland in 1979) the population is prepared to accept this method of fund raising. Many central cities have already instituted payroll taxes on all incomes earned within the city, regardless of the residential location of the worker. This method attempts to regain for the city income earned within its boundaries by wage earners who "use" the infrastructure and facilities of the city to make a living but reside and pay local taxes in another municipality. The problem with these methods of obtaining additional revenue is that they (1) incur greater tax costs on the inhabitants of the older urban areas and (2) can act as a detriment to the location of business activities within their boundaries. These issues, which are related to the geographical base of the taxes, lead to the next section.

Structural Responses to Local Government Fragmentation

The large number of governmental units existing in North American major urban regions is not of itself intrinsically bad, for the issues arise not over the numbers themselves but the efficiency with which they perform their tasks. This efficiency has to be determined with respect to the size of jurisdiction over which they might best operate and the degree of coordination required with other local government activities. Ideally, small jurisdictions should do what they do best, and large jurisdictions should deal with those urban functions that they do best. The response to the fragmented local government issue, therefore, involves consideration of (1) the type of functions and services that are most efficiently provided by different sizes of jurisdictions and (2) the form of local government structure that is best suited to provide the range of urban functions and services. Though there are no specific answers to these particular considerations, there is sufficient evidence to provide a response.

Community Size and Urban Functions. In a detailed examination of the literature concerning the size of population that is most suitable for the support of particular urban functions and services, Hallman[17] came to the conclusion that three different community sizes were commonly mentioned. These are: (1) small, involving neighborhoods and small municipalities up to a population of about 40,000; (2) intermediate, including central cities, some large municipalities and urban counties, containing populations up to 200,000–250,000; and (3) area wide, involving the entire urban region or metropolis, and which can well contain a population up to a few million. These size ranges are obviously very broad, and they suggest quite wide ranges in the populations that are best suited to the support of particular functions and services.

The decisions concerning the allocations of functions and services to these three sizes of community are based on the size that is best suited to the support of these activities as revealed in economy of scale studies, and the degree to which close interaction is required with the population being served. The close interaction constraint means that urban functions and services are allocated to the smallest size of urban community possible, given the range of populations suggested by the economy of scale literature. The outcome of these decisions is presented in Table 5.5, though in most cases the allocation is to a particular size community, and in a number of instances two levels of governmental jurisdiction may be appropriate. For example, building permits and building inspection services are provided ideally at the small-scale level, but they can also be provided with a reasonable level of efficiency and service sensitivity at the intermediate level. Police services, though best provided at the smallest scale so that there might be greater possibilities for direct contact with the public, must also be provided for the metropolis as a whole. In these cases, the higher level jurisdiction would be

Table 5.5. A theoretical allocation of urban functions and services to three different sizes of community within a metropolitan area.

Small	Intermediate	Large
Social services		
Elementary education		
Refuse collection		
Water sales		
Street cleaning		
Comm. rec. facilities		
Snow removal	Snow removal	
Parking lots	Parking lots	
Building permits	Building permits	
Building inspection	Building inspection	
Housing redevelopment	Housing redevelopment	
Secondary education	Secondary education	
	Housing (low income, elderly)	
	Fire protection	
	Ambulance services	
	Hospitals	Hospitals
	Vocational training	Vocational training
		Refuse disposal
		Sewage disposal
		Water treatment & trunk lines
		Airports and ports
		Bus and truck terminals
		Railroads and railyards
		Mass transit
		Transport planning
		Cultural facilities
		Regional parks
		Planning and land use control
		Building codes and regulations
Police		Police
Health services		Health services
Welfare		Welfare

[a]Low income, elderly.

Table compiled from the detailed discussion of the economics of scale for urban functions literature in Hallman (1977), pp. 182-194.

responsible for the coordination of the service to assure adequate provision for all parts of the metropolitan area.

Education services are more difficult to allocate in the U.S. than Canada, for efficiency and community interaction constraints are not the only requirements for the provision of the service. In the U.S., matters involving integration are equally as important, and may even override the economy of scale and community interaction concerns. This is not meant to imply that schools organized within large jurisdictions suffer severe diseconomies of scale, for they may not, but it is meant to suggest that the addition of different criteria can change the most appropriate size of community for the function or service involved. In the case of elementary and secondary education, sometimes the best way to achieve racially balanced schools is to organize the system for the largest jurisdiction possible, rather than the smallest.

Structure of Local Government. One of the most interesting implications from Table 5.5 is with respect to the structure of local governments. Most local governments are of the one-tier variety, operating all the functions and services that they provide over their prescribed jurisdiction. The "best" allocation of functions and services represented in Table 5.5, however, implies that some functions and services are most appropriately provided in small-scale operations for local areas, while another group are most appropriately provided at the larger scale for entire urban regions or metropolitan areas. The intermediate group contains a number of activities, but all except three of these overlap with either those allocated to the local scale or at the large scale. Thus, the theoretical allocation, based on individual economy of scale studies and the need for interaction, suggest a two-tier form of local government structure. One tier, at the local level, would be involved with those activities requiring a great deal of community involvement and interaction, and another tier would be concerned with those requiring large-scale operations in order to be provided most economically.

This has been recognized in many metropolitan areas in Canada and the U.S., though the method by which two-tier local government has been implemented varies quite significantly. The most common form, as has been discussed in the preceding chapter, involves the establishment of either single-function or multi-function special districts to offer a particular service, or related set of services, over an entire metropolitan or county area. The special district response, however, is one of the direct causes of excessive fragmentation and insularity in local government, for the bodies act independently of each other and are frequently not coordinated by an elected organization. Two other responses to this apparent need for a two-tier form of organization, that provide a greater level of coordination between municipalities and also possibilities for more direct public involvement, are those involving unification and federation.

Unification and Federation. Unification has been the method of governmental consolidation adopted most frequently by metropolitan areas in the U.S. It typically involves the reallocation of responsibility for certain functions from all municipalities to the county level, and the funding of these activities by the entire region. In this way, the county forms a single metropolitan government and looks after area-wide issues, while the local governments operate those activities that can be provided efficiently at a smaller scale of operation and require closer community involvement. Unfortunately, this form of restructuring has occurred in only a few cases, for the complexity of the legal processes involved has confined such reorganization to those few cases where the metropolitan area lies almost exclusively in a single county. There are seven examples of county metropolitan government in the U.S., and in only one does unification extend beyond the core county.

There are very few examples of municipal/county consolidation in the major urban regions of the U.S. because of the political difficulties involved in unification and the reallocation of functions. The first difficulty concerns reaching agreement between the municipalities and county involved with respect to the form of organization, political representation, and the reallocation of functions and services. If this initial round of discussions, often involving local plebiscites, results in agreement, then the second round can be equally as tedious. This requires the agreement by the state for the county to adopt an enlarged governmental role, and the agreement may have to take the form of an amendment to the state constitution to be voted on by all constituents within the state. These procedures can take a number of years and involve so many groups and expensive hearings that the process itself becomes the greatest barrier to any reorganization.

Federation is similar to the one-county concept, and in the case of a one-county metropolitan area the two may be indistinguishable. Federation allows two- and even three-tiered local governments to occur in situations where the metropolitan region spreads over a number of counties and municipalities. The idea of federated metropolitan areas has been an appealing one in the U.S. and Canada since the establishment of the London County Council in England in 1888/89, but in the U.S. various attempts (Boston, 1896; Oakland, 1921; Pittsburgh, 1929) all ended in failure. The only example of a near federated form of municipal government in the U.S. is Dade County (Miami), where a two-tier form of government for the incorporated municipalities and a one-tier metropolitan government for the unincorporated parts of the county were approved in 1957. De facto federation has evolved in Nassau County (New York) as a number of functions have been transferred to the county government over a period of time.

The most extensive effort for the reorganization of local government within the federation framework has occurred within the Ontario portion of the Windsor–Quebec City major urban region. The government of the Province of Ontario has initiated and implemented widespread local government reform and the allocation of specific functions to different levels of government, mostly within a two-tier framework, commencing with the establishment of Metro Toronto in 1954. Ten other forms of regional government were established between 1969 and 1974 (Fig. 5.1). Most of these are clustered in the rapidly urbanizing part of the province around Toronto, one involves a dispersed area of recreational homes where regional planning and environmental protection is required (Muskoka), and another embraces the region around Ottawa.

Apart from reorganization and amalgamation at the local level, which in the case of Metro Toronto involved the consolidation of 13 municipalities into 6 units of local government to form the lowest tier, the most important issue concerns the

Fig. 5.1. Location of regional government units in the Ontario portion of the Windsor–Quebec City major urban region.

way in which the service and administrative functions are allocated among the three levels of government (local, regional or metro, and provincial). A summary of the allocations implemented for six of the regions is presented in Table 5.6. Although there are differences in the allocations among the regions, for each one is considered as a special case with its own preferences, there is a remarkable degree of uniformity in the allocation of activities. Generally, the regions (or metro) are responsible for the major services, such as police, water, sewers, social services, and borrowing, whereas the municipalities deal with such matters as zoning, garbage collection, and parks. Provincial subsidies and grants are allocated to the regional councils on a formula basis, and the councils are responsible for the disbursement of the funds.

The most important feature of this reorganization concerns not, however, the details of the restructuring or the allocation of the functions and services, but the role of the provincial government. In the Canadian political system, the provinces can exert a leadership role in the reorganization of local government, and, if the local politicans and community are reluctant to cooperate, it can foster cooperation with financial inducements. This reluctance is often based upon a misunderstanding of the changing role of local government, and is led by local politicians who fear an erosion of their power base. None of the areas has been reorganized without considerable local involvement and numerous studies of the benefits and costs that may be incurred. These evaluations are continuing as the regional governments establish themselves and initial bureaucratic diseconomies are resolved.

Radical Responses to Issues Involving Metropolitan Finance and Organization

The radical response suggests that the structural reforms outlined in the previous section involve mere structural tinkering and fail to deal directly with the

Table 5.6. Allocation of administrative and service functions between the local, regional, and provincial levels of government in the Ontario portion of the Windsor–Quebec City urban axis.

Functions	Metro Toronto	Ottawa-Carleton	Niagara	York	Muskoka	Waterloo
Borrowing	R*	R	R	R	R	R
E. M. O.	R	R	R	R	R	R
General welfare	R	R	R	R	R	R
Child welfare	R	R	R	R	R	R
Homes for the aged	R	R	R	R	R	R
Juvenile Court (costs by order)	R	R	R	R	R	R
Nursing services and day nurseries (costs)	R	S	R	R	R	R
Anatomy Act	R	S	R	R	R	R
Health Unit	L*	R	R	R	R	R
War veterans burial	R	L	R	R	R	R
Sanatoria for consumptives	S*	S	R	R	R	R
Homes for the retarded (costs	R	L	S	S	S	R
Water supply	S	R	S	S	L	S
Tax Levy	S	S	S	S	S	S
Sewage	S	S	S	S	S	S
Planning	S	S	S	S	S	S
Roads	S	S	S	S	S	S
Traffic	S	S	S	S	S	S
Grants to hospitals	S	S	S	S	S	S
Parking	S	S	S	S	L	S
Police	R	L	S	R	P*	R
Public transit	R	L	L	L	L	R
Parks	S	L	L	S	L	L
Tax collection	L	L	L	L	L	L
Gas and electricity distribution	L	L	L	L	L	L
Library	L	L	L	L	L	S
Recreation and community centres	L	L	L	L	L	L
Solid waste	S	L	L	L	L	S
Fire protection	L	L	L	L	L	L
Ambulance service	R	L	L	L	L	L
Sidewalks	L	L	L	L	L	L

*Codes: S–shared, R–regional, L–local, P–provincial, ^acosts.
Source: Yeates (1975), p. 287.

fundamental issues involving the redistributive effects of decisions made in both the public and private sectors.[18] But, just as there is a range of responses from those suggesting structural reforms, so is there a range of responses from those promoting more radical solutions. In this section, attention will be devoted to two of these radical responses. One involves the responses made within mixed capitalist-socialist systems, and the other involves a more socialist response.

Response Within Mixed Capitalist-Socialist Systems. The first response involves the recognition that the problems facing individual municipalities cannot really be resolved either within their own borders or at the level of some kind of amalgamated metropolitan region. This is because the changes that have to be made to resolve the issues involve a reordering of national priorities and control over public and private investment decisions. As a consequence, actions by the government at the highest level are required, for these are not changes that can be made by a single metropolis or group of metropolises.

The matter of the reordering of national priorities has been touched upon in the previous section on fiscal responses with respect to the transfer of responsibilities. In the context of the response within mixed capitalist-socialist systems, however, the issue becomes more than that of merely identifying matters that are of national concern and for which municipalities cannot be expected to pay. In this approach, the response is based on a fundamental recognition of the role of the state in providing equal access to health care, social services, reasonable quality housing, education, etc. Under such a system, health care would be nationalized, there would be extensive investment by the national state government in housing construction and urban redevelopment, and the central government would also be responsible for the provision of social services and ensuring equality of access to education. The primary source of revenue to pay for these services, and also to provide the money for fiscal transfers to the municipalities, would be quite steep progressive taxes on incomes, profits, capital gains, and inheritances (or death duties).

One of the basic causes of problems facing metropolises lies in the decentralization of jobs and economic activities. The radical response would support the economic control perspective discussed previously, and contend that the prime reason for this is a lack of control or influence by the state over the location decisions made by the owners of capital. To prevent the lack of balanced growth and the inequities that result from such decisions in a capitalist economy, the response within a mixed capitalist-socialist system would be to use public investments to counteract the trends, and various instruments that can be used by the state to influence the location decisions of private investors. These instruments could involve licensing the location of certain types of activities in particular areas, and differential levels of profits taxes according to the needs for employment generation in the various parts of the major urban regions.

A Socialist Response. This second radical approach is rooted much more directly in the class interpretation of the capitalist state, which has been discussed previously with respect to qualitative and quantitative efficiency and the control exercised by capitalists. This response would contend that the owners of capital, and those who have effective control of the decision-making powers of corporations, seek to perpetuate their dominant position over those who do not. In the context of urbanism, these positions of dominance, which give rise to social classes in the population, can be enhanced and protected by the current structure of municipal finances and the fragmentation of local government.

There are many examples of the way in which these positions can be enhanced by the present organization of local government in North America, but perhaps three will suffice. First, the fragmentation of political units and the search by municipalities for the most productive tax base allow businesses that are in demand to play off one jurisdiction against another, and gain certain advantages, such as exclusion from planning or building code by-laws. Business activities that are not in demand can, on the other hand, be excluded from certain municipalities by the raising of excessive property taxes or a change in the zoning by-laws. Thus the wealthier municipalities obtain the best commercial and manufacturing activities, and the poorer municipalities the worst.

Secondly, fragmentation allows for a geographic segmentation of social classes and also permits the higher class groups to consolidate their position. This can be witnessed most clearly with respect to schooling. The higher class segment of the population can predominate within a particular municipality through the construction of only expensive housing on large lots, attract a few high technology industries and good quality shopping centers to enhance the tax base, and thus provide good quality schooling through the large volume of revenue generated. The children of the municipality attend these schools and, because of the environment and quality of education, receive a better education than those attending schools in poorer municipalities. As a consequence, the upper classes are able to "stack the deck" in favor of perpetuating the position of the family in the class system, and at the same time ensuring that the family associates only with those in the same group.

The third example involves a special case of the more general situation described with respect to geographic segmentation and social classes alone. This special case involves an interpretaion of the role that has been created for the central city by outward migration of the upper and middle class, predominantly white, population from the central city. The result of this out-migration is that the central city in many North American cities, and particularly those in the Bosnywash, lower Great Lakes, and Ohio Valley major urban regions, has become a "container" of the under- and unemployed which, in the capitalist system, act as a disciplining mechanism on the labor force. Not only is the inner city the container for the reservoir of the unemployed, it has also become the reminder of the environment from which much of the work force has escaped, and apparently to which it does not wish to return.

This interpretation of the result of fragmented government and fiscal imbalance leads fairly clearly to a response based on the political economy of Marx and Engels.[19] The response is to encourage the creation of a classless society, which is considered to be the logical outcome of the class struggles which occur in capitalist societies. The creation of classes in a capitalist society results in a dialectical set of social relations, i.e., relations that are both reciprocal (one is either in a particular class or one is not) and antagonistic (because the members of one class are seeking to perpetuate domination over another). This dialectical set of relations results in conflict,[20] expressed most dramatically but not necessarily in a series of revolutions, which leads to eventual class synthesis.

The Most Likely Course of Events

The most likely course of events is, as mentioned at the beginning of this section, likely to continue to be within the structural framework. There are a number of reasons for this, the first having to do with the nature of the North American economic and political systems, and the second involving a general perception of radical approaches. There is no doubt, however, that in general the structural responses tend toward a form of urban government that is similar to that created via the capitalist-socialist form of response. This is because the structural responses tend toward a transfer of responsibilities to the higher levels of government within the state, and the exertion of greater influence by the higher levels of government on the location decisions of the corporations.

The North American economic and political systems seem to be capable of responding to the changes required by political urban issues within an evolutionary framework. Though the evolutionary process tends at times to be too slow, and definitely quite cumbersome, nevertheless an evolutionary development of responses does take place. Furthermore, the capitalist system has provided a fairly high standard of living and considerable freedoms for the large majority of the population, and so the evolutionary process is much preferred. Revolutionary responses lead to uncontrolled situations, and in uncontrolled situations one can never be too sure of the outcome.

This general favor for the evolutionary process is enhanced by the critical perception of the practice of many socialist societies. Although radical theories often sound persuasive within the context of a general critique of capitalist societies, it is difficult not to note the apparent difficulty of putting socialist theories into practice. It is quite apparent, for example, that countries adopting these theories do not have classless societies. In particular, it is evident that one class system (economic) tends to be replaced by another based on influence within the bureaucracy which controls society. Furthermore, the more radical interpretation of the inner city/outer city question provides a rather simple explanation for a rather complex phenomenon, for, as has been noted in Chapter 4, not all inner cities exhibit the same characteristics, and neither are there similar levels of disparity.

RESPONSES TO ISSUES CONCERNING THE URBAN CONSUMPTION OF RURAL LAND

Probably the most important influence on the level of response to the issue of the urban consumption of rural land involves the notion of "individual rights." In North America, these rights seem to involve (1) property rights, (2) life-style preferences, (3) space-territory feelings, and (4) accessibility and service demands.[21] Property rights are probably the best known rights sanctified by law and custom in North America. In general, they include the rights of an individual or group to own land and to do whatever they wish with that land. Although this level of theoretical freedom is curtailed by local ordinances and zoning, the right to own property and realize the material and nonmaterial benefits of ownership are, subject to certain legal constraints, quite sacrosanct. Furthermore, these rights of property ownership are supported by the vast majority of the North American population, and so the response to the rural-urban land conversion issue is severely limited by this political reality.

The rural-urban land conversion issue is also constrained to varying degrees by the other three "rights" mentioned above. Life-style preferences, particularly those involving second-home recreational developments, are now becoming quite widely accepted, though the environmental impacts have become matters of concern in some areas (e.g., Big Sur, Calif.). In fact, environmental questions are more of a public concern in most areas than the removal of agricultural land. Space-territory feelings, as expressed by the desire of most of the population to own a certain amount of private geographical space, are, in effect, recognized by housing programs designed to increase the rate of home ownership. These feelings appear to be expressed most clearly in desire for single-family homes, even by singles or young marrieds with no children. The fourth right involves the apparent acceptance of the notion that, regardless of where they are living, people should have a level of access and local services that are similar to those they might experience in urban areas.

The identification of these preferences, and the recognition that in North American society they appear to have become accepted as individual rights, help to explain why the public policy response is to permit fairly high levels of land consumption for urban purposes. There are, however, certain rights that are ignored in the above discussion. One of these concerns the right of individuals who would like to but cannot take advantage of the rights and would like to exercise similar preferences. Another involves the rights of future generations, particularly with respect to agricultural land for the production of food, and some unspoiled amenity and recreational locations.

Thus, the response has to be evaluated in terms of these conflicting "rights," and experiences in Canada, with respect to the consumption of agricultural land, are quite interesting in this regard. Two experiences will be discussed briefly, the first involving attempts to protect agricultural land in the lower Fraser Valley portion of the N.W. and B.C. major urban region, and the second involves the Niagara fruit belt area of the Windsor–Quebec City major urban region.

Response in British Columbia

The area around Vancouver and its suburbs in the southwest portion of British Columbia is one of Canada's fastest growing areas. The pace of growth and immigration from the rest of Canada have been so great during the past two decades that the provincial government is attempting to resist the movement of people to the area, though it is difficult for it to do so in an open society. The population growth has resulted in the spread of population and industrial activity over some of

Canada's richest farmland in the part of the country that is climatically most suitable for the production of fruits and vegetables as well as other crops. During the period 1954/1972, the rate of conversion to urban uses was estimated to be about 10,000 acres per year.[22] In response to the need to preserve agricultural land, the government adopted a Land Commission Act in 1973.

The B.C. Land Commission Act has four major objectives: (1) the preservation of agricultural land for farm use; (2) the establishment of a zone of greenbelt lands around the larger urban areas, and particularly Vancouver; (3) the creation of a land bank to provide sufficient land to accommodate future urban and industrial growth at reasonable land prices; and (4) the establishment of a parkland reserve and the creation of parks for recreational use. The most important function of the Commission, and its only area of regulatory power, is with respect to its power to designate land as agricultural and the procedure which could be followed to appeal against such designation. Land maps of agricultural preserve areas were prepared, in conjunction with the B.C. Department of Agriculture, and the final designations were made following lengthy public hearings. Given the structure of appeals, it is evident that the strength of the Commission depends upon the independence of Commission members (who are appointees of the provincial government) and the support given by the government.

In the public discussions preceding implementation of the Act, the property rights of the farmers who owned the land involved dominated most of the debate. Farmers close to expanding urban areas were opposed to the Act because their properties would decline in value if purchasers could not envisage immediate or future urban development possibilities. Farmers living some distance from urban areas, whose land was not likely to increase in value as a result of urban encroachment, were more likely to be in favor of the Act. One of these chief contentions of the opponents of the Act was that it not only violated the rights of owners to do what they wished with their property, but that farmers could realize adequate retirement income only through the sale of their land. Anything that would constrain land values would, as a consequence, remove potential retirement income from farmers.

The political impact of the Act in British Columbia has been quite interesting. The party in power (NDP) who implemented the Act was replaced in 1975 by a more conservative, pro-development, government (Social Credit). In October 1976, the government removed all but one of the NDP appointees to the Commission, and the general impression was that the new group would approve more rural-urban land conversion applications. In politics, impressions often speak louder than acts, and, although this impression persists, the post-1976 actions of the Commission would suggest that it is being reasonably vigilant in resisting applications for de-designation. Perhaps the Commission and the government in power are recognizing that the general climate of public opinion is in favor of actions which limit urban growth and attempt to preserve the better agricultural lands for future generations. There are, however, recent signs of more approvals of land conversion applications by the Cabinet of the Provincial Government than might be expected.

Response to the Niagara Fruit Belt Issue

The amount of land with soil and climatic conditons suitable for the production of tender fruit crops (peaches, cherries, pears, prunes, plums, grapes, etc.) in Canada is limited to the area around the lower Fraser Valley and a small portion of the Niagara Peninsula in Ontario. As the Niagara Peninsula is in the heart of Canada's most populated area, the region is particularly important because it has a high level of accessibility to the bulk of the market. The most extensive acreage of fruit production was achieved in the Niagara Peninsula in 1951 (53,200 acres) and since that time urban expansion has removed 20% of the land from tender fruit productio. [23] Given the scarcity in the availability of land of this type, the response to urban encroachment in this area is fascinating.

Although the actions of the B.C. Land Commission have not gone unnoticed in Ontario, there has been little or no government response to the issue. The provincial government, in effect, used the formation of a regional government unit in this area to side-step the question, and passed the responsibility for preserving agricultural lands to the regional and local government. By so doing, the influence of the local landowner is magnified, and the right to hold property for speculative purposes is preserved rather than the rights of future generations for Canadian grown tender fruits. Furthermore, actions being considered by the provincial government, such as the Food Land Guidelines for Municipalities, contain no requirements for action.

In this particular case, it appears that the rights of the property owners are considered to be of paramount importance, and the desire by the provincial government for the preservation of these rights supersedes other considerations. Although the pressure on the lands in the fruit-belt area do not now appear to be as great in the future as was thought in the early 1970s, nevertheless it is predicted that the population in the Regional Municipality of Niagara will increase by about 43,000 between 1976 and 2001. With the lack of strong governmental direction, the responses appear to be for either (1) allowing the land to be consumed or (2) maintaining some sort of control of land consumption. The first alternative is a free market approach, and it envisages greater imports of fruits from Mexico and the U.S. south and west in the future.

The second approach requires careful implementation at the local and regional government level. There are substantial parts of the urban areas of the Niagara Peninsula that remain undeveloped but are surrounded by urban development. These lands are essentially lost to agriculture, and should be developed before agricultural lands are rezoned for other purposes. [24] In some cases, when farms do come on to the market it may be possible to follow the action of Suffolk County (Long Island), where urban areas have been transferred to urban uses at a rapid rate in recent years. This action involves the purchase of title or development rights to farmland by the county and the leasing by the county of land to farmers. This way, the county hopes to ensure sufficient open space to provide a habitable environment for future generations. Also, farmers can be discouraged from selling by ensuring higher prices for their products through the means of greater protective tariffs. Protective tariffs have to be implemented by the federal government, and the implementation of such protective policies involves a wide array of internal and external political trade-offs.

The various issues discussed in this chapter cannot therefore be discussed in a vacuum, for all urban issues are affected by governmental actions. As a consequence, no solution is simple, and all the responses involve some degree of action or inaction by the state. The course of the action that is taken depends on the strength of influence exerted by a mélange of interests, ranging from the corporate through to various pressure groups formed by the electorate. The responses that are pursued to become public policy, and are eventually formulated into programs, depend upon the degree to which the importance of the issue is recognized, and the political philosophies that are considered as capable of providing answers. The responses must be articulated with respect to these political philosophies because the decisions that are made, and have to be made, are political decisions. It is, therefore, impossible to ignore the role of the state and the ideologies of the various pressure groups in the formulation of these decisions.

NOTES

[1] J. C. Corbett, "Canadian Cities: How 'American' Are They?," *Urban Affairs Quarterly*, Vol. 13, 3 (1978), pp. 383–394.

[2] P. A. Lupsha and W. J. Siembieda, "The Poverty of Public Services in the Land of Plenty: An Analysis and Interpretation" in D. C. Perry and A. J. Watkins (eds.), *The Rise of the Sunbelt Cities* (Beverly Hills: Sage Publications, Urban Affairs Annual Reviews, Vol. 14, 1977).

[3] B. M. Moriarty, "A Note on Unexplained Residuals in North-South Wage Differentials," *Journal of Regional Science*, Vol. 18, 1 (1978), pp. 105–108.

[4] J. Cannon, "Government Impact on Industrial Location" in L. Collins and D. F. Walker (eds.), *Locational Dynamics of Manufacturing Activity* (New York: John Wiley & Sons, 1975).

[5] W. D. Angel, "To Make a City: Entrepreneurship on the Sunbelt Frontier" in D. C. Perry and A. J. Watkins (eds.), *The Rise of the Sunbelt Cities* (Beverly Hills: Sage Publications, Urban Affairs Annual Reviews, Vol. 14, 1977, pp. 109–128).

[6] A. R. Pred, *Major Job-Providing Organizations and Systems of Cities* (Washington, D.C.: Association of American Geographers, Resource Paper No. 27, 1974).

[7] G. A. Nader, *Cities of Canada, Vol. 2: Profiles of Fifteen Metropolitan Centres* (Toronto: Macmillan of Canada).

[8] R. B. Cohen, "Multinational Corporations, International Finance, and the Sunbelt" in D. C. Perry and A. J. Watkins (eds.), *The Rise of the Sunbelt Cities* (Beverly Hills, Calif.: Sage Publications, Urban Affairs Annual Reviews, Vol. 14, 1977).

[9] D. M. Gordon, "Capitalist Development and the History of American Cities" in W. K. Tabb and L. Sawers (eds.), *Marxism and the Metropolis* (New York: Oxford University Press, 1978, pp. 25–63).

[10] G. Sternlieb and J. W. Hughes, "New Regional and Metropolitan Realities of America," *Journal of the American Institute of Planners*, July (1977), pp. 227-234.

[11] P. A. Morrison, "Current Demographic Changes in Regions of the United States" (Santa Monica, Calif.: The Rand Corporation, 1977, P-6000).

[12] B. D. McDowell (ed.), *A Look to the North: Canadian Regional Experience*, Advisory Commission on Intergovernmental Relations, 1974.

[13] W. K. Tabb, "The New York City Fiscal Crisis" in W. K. Tabb and L. Sawers (eds.), *Marxism and the Metropolis* (New York: Oxford University Press, 1978, pp. 241-266).

[14] R. Wade, "The End of the Self-Sufficient City: New York's Fiscal Crisis in History," *Urbanism Past and Present*, Winter (1976-77), pp. 1-4.

[15] Ibid., p. 3.

[16] G. Carey, "Land Tenure, Speculation, and the State of the Aging Metropolis," *Geographical Review*, Vol. 66 (1976), pp. 253-265.

[17] H. W. Hallman, *Small and Large Together: Governing the Metropolis* (Beverly Hills: Sage Publications, 1977).

[18] D. Harvey, *Social Justice and the City* (Baltimore: Johns Hopkins Press, 1973); and P. J. Ashton, "The Political Economy of Suburban Development" in W. K. Tabb and L. Sawers (eds.), *Marxism and the Metropolis* (N.Y.: Oxford University Press, 1978).

[19] K. Marx and F. Engels, *Collected Works, Vols. 1-9* (N.Y.: International Publishers, 1975). These are reprints of the writings of Marx and Engels published originally in a variety of places during the 1840s.

[20] K. Cox (ed.), *Urbanization and Conflicts in Market Societies* (Chicago: Maaroufa, 1977).

[21] L. H. Russwurm, *The Surroundings of Our Cities: Problems and Planning Implications of Urban Fringe Landscapes* (Ottawa: Community Planning Press, 1977).

[22] C. Baubien and R. Tabacnik, *People and Agricultural Land* (Ottawa: Science Council of Canada).

[23] R. R. Krueger, "Urbanization of the Niagara Fruit Belt," *The Canadian Geographer*, Vol. 22, 3 (1978), pp. 179-194.

[24] Kreuger, op. cit.

Chapter 6

Future growth among the major urban regions

It is always difficult to predict the course of future trends, for there are so many events that can influence growth and the distribution of population. Thus, although this chapter focusses on the likely future distribution of population among the major urban regions, there is also some discussion of ongoing trends that are and could influence the growth (or decline) of some of the regions quite dramatically. A predicted distribution of population among the major urban regions is developed from quite simple considerations, and most of these considerations have been discussed in the preceding chapters. The forecasts for each region are really to be regarded as guidelines to indicate what "might be" if current demographic and interregional migration trends persist. Along with this discussion of future trends is an examination of the nonmetropolitan growth phenomenon, which has been particularly evident during the 1970s.

POPULATION GROWTH IN NORTH AMERICA

One of the most important benchmarks against which population predictions for individual urban regions must be compared is the estimate of the future total population of North America as a whole. The estimate that has been selected is based on projections prepared by the U.S. Bureau of the Census[1] and Statistics Canada.[2] These projections assume that the birthrate during the remainder of the present century will remain at only a fraction above the replacement level, and that levels of net immigration will average about 60,000 per year to Canada and 400,000 per year to the U.S. Although these levels of immigration are obviously subject to great fluctuations and, in the case of the U.S., may well understate the time volume of immigration in any one year by a considerable amount, they have to be regarded as reasonable average estimates over a few decades.

The other two factors that influence the general rate of population increase are trends in the death rate and the demographic structure of the population. The effect of these components of population growth are easier to examine because trends in the death rate have been fairly consistent over time, the number of people who will be elderly 20 years from now is already known, as is the age profile of the population who will be of child-bearing age during the next two decades. The average length of life will continue to increase, and the proportion of the population in the older age groups by the years 2000/01 will be much greater than that currently existing. Consequently, the actual number of older people will be larger. Furthermore, females born during the "baby-boom" years are now reaching child-bearing age, and there is no sign that the decrease in the fertility rate will be halted, let alone reversed, in the short term. During the 1990s, the actual number of new births will, as a consequence, be much lower, than those born during the "baby-bust" years of the late 1960s and 1970s begin to reach child-bearing age.

As a consequence, the volume of population in Canada and the U.S. will increase throughout the rest of the century but at a decreasing rate. By the year 2001, the population of Canada is likely to be about 30.6 million and the population of the U.S. in the year 2000 about 260.4 million. Thus, the population of North America as a whole will probably increase by 23% during the last quarter of the century, as compared with the 43% increase experienced during the third quarter. The absolute increment will, however, be greater, for the total population is likely to increase 55 million during the fourth quarter as compared with the 50 million increase during the third. The actual level of demands for housing, jobs, urban infrastructure, food, services, etc., of this fourth quarter increment will, therefore, increase at a level similar to that required by the third quarter increment. Furthermore, the impact of these demands is likely to be concentrated to a great extent within the major urban regions.

The implications of this volume of increase are quite salutory, particularly as the range of demands is likely to be different. During the third quarter of the present century, the increase was mainly the result of the high post-war birth rate, and the impact of the large number of young people was evidenced most clearly in the demand for educational facilities and in the need for the creation of new employment opportunities. The impact of the 55 million increase likely to occur during the fourth quarter will arise from the aging of the population as a whole. The prevalence of a generally older population will be felt in a variety of ways, such as in the demand for health care facilities, better pension schemes, and the demand for better planned housing for those physically impaired. Intriguingly, the youth "confrontations" of the 1960s and early 1970s could well be echoed in the 1990s by "middle-aged" neuroses and diseases, as manifested by high rates of alcoholism and even higher rates of divorce than those existing at present.

A PROBABLE DISTRIBUTION OF POPULATION
IN THE YEARS 2000/01

Given these continent-wide trends, it is quite evident that the rate of growth of population in the major urban regions will decrease quite dramatically during the fourth quarter of the century, even though the volume of population will increase by a large amount. Accompanying this lower rate of population growth will be (1) a persisting shift of population to nonmetropolitan areas; (2) a continuing decrease in the proportion of the population of the continent that is located within the major urban regions; (3) considerable variation in growth rates as a result of interregional migration; which will be manifested by (4) higher rates of growth in the southern and western urban regions as compared with the others. Although the actual population to be located in the defined major urban regions in the years 2000/01 is difficult to predict, because of the variability of migration flows and the unpredictable forces that influence the birthrate, some indication of the likely numbers can be determined from the trends graphed in Figure 6.1.

Some Growth Scenarios for the Major Urban Regions

The highest rates of growth during the last quarter of the present century are likely to be experienced by the major urban regions of Florida, the Northwest and British Columbia, the Gulf Shore, and California. The major influences on the volume of migration to Florida, involving those seeking a pleasant climate in which to retire, or employment in recreational and associated service activities, are likely to increase in importance in the near future. Not only is the population of the continent aging, but longer vacations mean more time for recreational activities, and smaller families imply a greater availability of discretionary funds for spending on such activities. This increase in population within the urban region generates a high level of local demand for consumer products, and this local demand serves to attract manufacturing industries to the region.

Similarly, the Pacific Northwest and British Columbia urban region are located in an area which is attractive for retirees and those on vacation, but there are also other compelling reasons for predicting growth within the region. First of all, the economic base of the region is quite diverse, ranging from industries associated with the high technology aeronautics industry to those derived from the extensive local resources of the region and its hinterland. These resources have given rise to a flourishing array of industrial activities based on wood and pulp processing as well as the refining of oil and the utilization of natural gas. In the future, the geographical position of the region vis-à-vis Japan and the Asian continent is likely to be even more important for trans-Pacific trade, and industries associated with this trade will undoubtedly be an even greater generator of growth. Although trade with China seems to be developing slowly at present, there is little doubt that tremendous opportunities exist for growth over the next few decades, and this urban region has the geographical location and resources to attract a considerable volume of business.

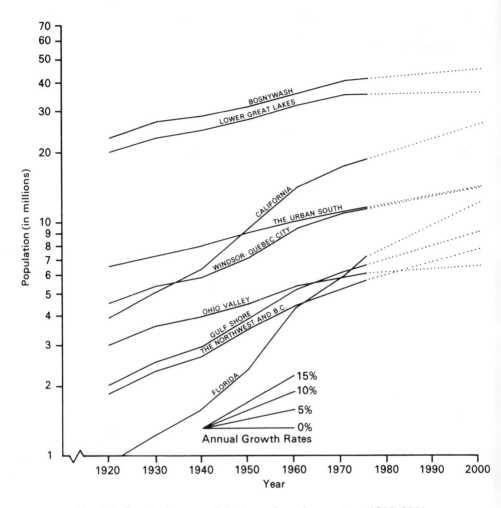

Fig. 6.1. Population growth in the major urban regions, 1920–2000.

Predicting the future growth of California is rather more difficult than the rather optimistic views expressed with respect to the Florida and the Pacific Northwest and British Columbia. On the one hand, California is becoming somewhat crowded, and the diseconomies of congestion on the highways and metropolitan sprawl, resulting in high per capita energy use, may well dampen the existing growth forces. On the other hand, the emphasis on high technology manufacturing, the location of the region vis-à-vis trans-Pacific markets, and the large local market which acts as an incubator for new industrial activities all point to a high level of local growth in the near future. Furthermore, the agricultural resources of the farmland within the region cannot be ignored because the production is of a high-value nature, and often involves a considerable level of local processing before being transported to markets elsewhere.

Predictions for the major urban region along the Gulf Shore are rather more hazardous to make than for the regions discussed in the preceding paragraphs. This is because there are a variety of forces of a positive and negative nature that could affect the economic future of the region quite dramatically. There is no doubt that the prime geographic location of growth within the region is the Houston area, for New Orleans is not a focus of dynamic economic activity. The growth forces within the Houston region are based on its involvement in oil, the petrochemical industry, and high technology industries that received considerable impetus from the establishment of the Manned Space Center within the area. These activities are, however, dependent upon a unique combination of political and financial forces that focus on the Houston area, and, as other regions within the U.S. realize the comparative shift in industrial activity that has occurred as a result of these political and financial forces, there may be some attempt to reduce their importance. Nevertheless, the cumulative impetus of aggressive entrepreneurship associated with a favorable industry-mix will undoubtedly result in a relatively high rate of growth within the region for the next decade or so.

Two major urban regions, the Windsor–Quebec City axis and the "urban" south, are likely to grow at about, or a little less than, the average rate of growth of the population in the continent as a whole. The urban region between Windsor and Quebec City grew at a rapid rate between 1950 and 1975, but there are now quite strong forces in favor of growth in western Canada which are being accompanied by significant shifts in the location of headquarter offices and financial activities within the axis. The considerable investments in and tax royalties received from the petroleum industry (as is demonstrated by the establishment of the Alberta Heritage Fund) are resulting in high rates of job creation in Alberta, and considerable spinoffs within the Vancouver region. Within the axis, the prospect of separation of Quebec from the Canadian federation has caused an exodus of certain headquarter offices and financial activities from Montreal, and the city is now becoming less integrated with the Canadian economy as a whole. Along with these trends, there is also the existence and likely continuation of a lower rate of immigration into Canada during the fourth quarter of the century than existed during the third. During much of the third quarter of the century, the net gain through immigration into Canada averaged almost 100,000 per year, with most of the immigrants locating in Toronto and Montreal. The influence of this component of population growth is likely to be reduced by about one-half during the fourth quarter, and many of the immigrants will select locations in the Toronto region or western Canada.

Whereas the "urban" south experienced a rate of growth that was somewhat less than the national average during the third quarter of the century, a growth rate at about the national average is predicted for the fourth quarter. Although this prediction and even the existence of a developing extensive urban region may be questioned, there is little doubt that the area has undergone considerable change in demographic structure and economic composition over the last few decades.

The "urban" south is part of an area that has been a net exporter of persons of working age for five decades up to 1970, but it is now apparent that this situation is being reversed.[3] The creation of new jobs in the Atlanta area and the establishment of textile and light manufacturing plants throughout the region have attracted an influx of labor. Furthermore, the construction of a highway network which links the area more closely with the east coast has facilitated industry interlinkages and the establishment of branch plants by major east coast companies within the region.

Examination of past growth trends leads to the suggestion that the Bosnywash, Lower Great Lakes, and Ohio Valley major urban regions will increase only slightly in population during the last quarter of the 20th century. The prevalence of older industries, and a dependence on highly capitalized manufacturing activities and an aging infrastructure, will continue to make these areas regions of relatively slow growth. Nevertheless, they will still contain a large portion of the population of the continent and many new market oriented firms will still choose to establish manufacturing plants within these regions. One factor that may alleviate the slow or no-growth situation is the present energy crisis. In contrast to the newer metropolises of the south and west, many of the older metropolises of the north and east do have flexible transport systems. They are not as dependent on the automobile for transport as the new cities, for they do have established public transport systems. Certainly, many of these systems require extensive new capital investment, and this capital investment will, of itself, be a generator of economic growth. Thus, although the population of these urban regions will grow at a rate far less than the continent average, public investment in the renewal of urban infrastructure may act as a stimulus to the economies of the regions and may help to alleviate the adverse industry-mix.

Predictions of the Populations of the Major Urban Regions in the Years 2000/01

The volume of population in the major urban regions by the years 2000/01 may, therefore, be of the order indicated in Table 6.1. Although the proportion of the population found in the major urban regions is predicted to decrease by two percentage points in the 25-year period, the actual number of people residing in these areas could well increase during the period by 30 million. Thus, the relative shift of population away from the major urban regions that was noticed in the first half of the 1970s is assumed to continue through to the end of the century. The information in Table 6.1 indicates, however, that this relative shift occurs almost entirely because of the exceeding low population increase that is predicted to occur in the Bosnywash and Lower Great Lakes urban regions. On the other hand, there will be a continuing relative shift of population toward the major urban regions of the south and west, and, by the year 2000, nearly 1 out of 10 North Americans will be residing in the California major urban region.

Of particular interest with respect to Canada is the prediction that the population of the Windsor–Quebec City axis will increase by only 2.5 million. This implies that the proportion of the population of the country residing within this

Table 6.1. Some extrapolations of the population of the major urban regions, 1975/2000.

Urban region	Population (in millions)		Population increase (%)		Distribution (%)	
	1975	2000	1950/1975	1975/2000	1975	2000
Bosnywash	44.4	48	36	8	18.8	16.5
Lower Great Lakes	37.6	39	31	4	15.9	13.4
California	19.7	28	100	42	8.4	9.6
The urban south	12.7	15	36	18	5.4	5.2
Windsor–Quebec City	12.5	15	71	20	5.3	5.2
Florida	7.4	13	229	76	3.2	4.5
The Gulf Shore	6.8	10	76	47	2.9	3.4
Ohio Valley	6.2	7	44	13	2.6	2.4
Northwest and B.C.	5.7	8	63	40	2.4	2.7
Total: urban regions	153	183	50	20	64.9	62.9
Total: U.S. and Canada	236	291	43	23	100.0	100.0

heartland area will decrease from 55% in 1976 to about 50% in 2001. The 1970s will, therefore, prove to be a "benchmark" decade in Canada, for it is during this period that the concentration of population in the heartland area reached a peak. The greatest share of this relative decline will occur in the Quebec portion of the region, for in this portion the fertility rate is now slightly below the replacement level. Furthermore, there is net out-migration from southern Quebec to the rest of Canada, and the Province is receiving very few immigrants. The impact of this decentralization of population away from the heartland will be felt most immediately in the political arena, for redistribution will alter significantly the geographic balance of power.

THE QUESTION OF NONMETROPOLITAN GROWTH

The decline in the proportion of the North American population located within the major urban regions is related to the growth of population in nonmetropolitan parts of the continent. In a study of population growth in nonmetropolitan counties in the U.S., that is, counties which do not have an urban nucleus of 50,000 or more people, Beale[4] demonstrates that whereas these counties were on the whole places of net out-migration prior to 1970, during the 1970s certain types of nonmetropolitan counties have become places of net in-migration. During the 1960/1970 decade, the population of nonmetropolitan counties in the U.S. increased by 4.4% as compared with an increase in the metropolitan counties of 17.1%. But, in the 1970/75 period, the population of the nonmetropolitan counties increased by 6.6% whereas that of the metropolitan counties increased by only 4.1%. Similarly, whereas the population of Canada residing in small centers of less than 10,000 population increased 6.3% during the 1971/76 period, the population of the country as a whole increased only 4.6% in the same five years.[5]

Types of Counties Involved in Nonmetropolitan Growth

Nonmetropolitan growth is focussed, both in Canada and the U.S., in certain types of counties. First, there are those immediately adjacent to metropolitan counties that had reasonably high rates of growth prior to 1970, and similar rates of increase during the 1970s as well. Growth in these areas is obviously related to the spreading out of metropolitan regions and the spread of exurbs into more remote agricultural and recreational areas. The interesting aspect of nonmetropolitan growth in the 1970s is, however, that whereas these were the prime areas of nonmetropolitan growth in the 1960s, other types of nonmetropolitan areas are increasing in population at a similar rate during the 1970s. These other types of nonmetropolitan areas can be described as those containing (1) post-secondary educational facilities, (2) retirement communities, and (3) new economic opportunities.

The rapid growth of post-secondary educational facilities after 1950 led to the rejuvenation of many small towns in nonmetropolitan areas. These small towns were usually the location of junior or community colleges, senior state colleges, and, in some cases, small universities. The rate of growth of these towns is directly related to the expansion of enrollment and the hiring of faculty to teach in the post-secondary facility, and it is interesting to note that places containing these facilities have continued to grow in population even though the educational facility may have entered a period of retrenchment. What appears to have happened is that the growth of the educational facility in the 1960s has generated the associated establishment of other services, urban infrastructure, some cultural activities, and a more pleasant social and recreational environment that has continued to attract small businesses, manufacturing plants, and hence migrants to the area. It is interesting to note that nonmetropolitan counties with senior state colleges in the U.S. grew at a faster rate between 1970 and 1975 than they did between 1960 and 1970.[6]

A number of small nonmetropolitan areas have experienced a high rate of growth because of heavy in-migration of people of retirement age. In the U.S., these nonmetropolitan retirement communities grew twice as fast between 1970 and 1975 than they did in the 1960s. In Canada, the migration patterns of the population above 60 years of age is directed toward not only the Canadian portion of the Northwest and British Columbia major urban region but also the smaller towns of rural British Columbia and the Maritime provinces. There are, perhaps, two behavioral processes and one economic process underlying these trends. One behavioral process involves a search for retirement locations in an equable climate with an unhurried safe small town environment. A second behavioral process is evident in the small number of retirees who return to their original home environment, as in the case of returnees from the Toronto area to small towns in the Maritimes. The third process involves a search for a low-cost living environment. Housing and the hiring of additional care services are usually cheaper in small towns than larger cities.

In a few cases, quite a dramatic recent nonmetropolitan growth has occurred as a result of new economic opportunities. Beale[7] quotes the cases of the recent development of oil fields in Duchesne County (Utah), natural gas in Sutton County (Texas), and coal mines in Rosebud County (Montana). Similar nonmetropolitan growth has occurred in association with the oil fields of northern Alberta and the natural gas areas of northwest British Columbia. Much of this growth in the western part of North America is based on the search for, and development of, sources of domestic energy, and there is every reason to suppose that this will be an ongoing activity for the rest of the 20th century. Certainly, the extensive coal fields of the U.S. and Canadian West require extensive development, and it may well prove feasible to replace many oil fueled and nuclear power generators by coal burning generators located in the western states and provinces.

Is it Just Nonmetropolitan Growth?

Although much of the discussion in the preceding section has been concerned with nonmetropolitan growth, the interesting aspect of urban change during the 1970s is the growth of middle-sized cities. SMSAs containing less than 500,000 people experienced a 7.5% population increase between 1970 and 1975, and CMAs of less than 500,000 incurred a similar population increase in the 1971 to 1976 period. The metropolitan areas that experienced declines in population, or little growth, were the largest metropolitan areas of all, and those that exhibited a decrease were the large metropolises of 3 million or more population in the U.S. Furthermore, the decreases in population that did occur tended to be in metropolitan areas within the Bosnywash and lower Great Lakes urban regions, though slow growth of large metropolises in other urban regions is noticeable. Thus, it is not just nonmetropolitan growth that is of interest, it is this phenomenon coupled with the relatively greater growth of middle-sized metropolises.

EXPLAINING THE RELATIVE DECLINE
OF LARGE METROPOLISES

Any examination of future population trends in North America must, therefore, take into account the forces that are leading to the deconcentration of the population into middle-sized and smaller communities. Metropolitan growth, in the past, was attributed to the superior economic advantages of larger cities. These economic advantages are often included in the phrase "external economies," for as cities grow the advantages of the big city location increase with the added presence of many other economic activities. The question of concern is, therefore, whether these big city advantages experienced in the past have now been offset by such disadvantages as to encourage people and business activities to locate elsewhere. These disadvantages are expressed most clearly in the form of congestion, pollution, and the fear of criminal acts. But, these negative attributes of metropolitan life are not unique to large urban areas, so there must be some other set of forces ecnouraging growth elsewhere in the urban system.

One aspect of these new forces that appears to cast some light on the new trends is that the migration decision is often noneconomic in nature. This is evidenced by the observation that two of the three types of nonmetropolitan growth counties discussed previously were essentially regions where there was no obvious economic base attracting jobs or people. The new forces may, therefore, be based on the changing locational preferences of people as well as the owners of capital or, to be more precise, the changing economic conditions that permit noneconomic considerations to become the greater influence. Perhaps North American society has now reached a situation where communications, transport, and the participation in cultural or recreational activities have now become so ubiquitous that large metropolises are no longer the only places where most economic and noneconomic activities can occur.

Thus, it may well be that for most people smaller metropolises, towns, and cities provide an environment which gives them access to jobs, recreational, and cultural activities that are sufficient for the kind of life that they wish to lead. Certainly, there will be many people for whom certain specific features of large metropolitan areas cannot be found in smaller places. For example, most small metropolises do not have the array of live cultural facilities found in the major metropolises. On the business side, it is still apparent that large corporations still choose to locate or maintain their headquarter offices in the larger metropolises, even though their production activities may be established in plants in much smaller places. There will, therefore, still continue to be certain elements of economic and cultural life that require metropolitan locations, but these have become fewer as what were once the advantages of metropolitan locations alone become more generally available over a large part of the North American continent.

The forces leading to the decline or nongrowth of the largest metropolitan areas may, however, be offset by social and economic factors that reinforce the importance of large places. Two examples of these may be sufficient to indicate the uncertain nature of predictions of future population distributions. On the sociological side, it is evident that the rapid expansion of female participation in the labor force and the reduction in size of the family mean that many locational choices are now constrained by the employment requirements of two wage-earners in a family rather than one. The probability of two persons finding satisfactory employment opportunities in a small town are significantly less than for larger places. As a consequence, this factor would tend to work in favor of population concentration in middle-sized and larger metropolises. On the economic side, increasing costs for fuel should eventually make public transportation more attractive to most people and could, theoretically, enhance the relative cost position of large cities with good public transport systems vis-à-vis smaller places that do not have such systems. Thus, some of the disadvantages of larger metropolitan areas may be offset by the existence of lower cost transportation.

SOME IMPLICATIONS OF THE POPULATION
AND REDISTRIBUTION TRENDS

The implications of the trends described in the previous sections are quite complex and, in this concluding section, they will be outlined briefly. Some of the implications are merely continuations of issues that are already of concern, while others are new in the sense that they are not now of widespread political importance. However, the political climate is so volatile that issues that appear dormant today often become matters of great public concern tomorrow. Two aspects of the macro-urban discussion should be emphasized. The first is that issues relating to major urban regions often fail to obtain the attention that they deserve simply because they involve a scale of analysis that is difficult to delimit. There are often no clear-cut boundaries to the effect of certain activities, such as those arising from air pollution. Secondly, the solutions to the problems usually involve many local jurisdictions, and as a consequence they become the responsibility of no one jurisdiction in particular.

The growth of population in the major urban regions of the south and west will, undoubtedly, result in greater levels of environmental decay and pollution. In this respect, they will begin to resemble some of the worst areas of the older industrial agglomerations of the lower Great Lakes and Bosnywash major urban regions. Already, a large portion of southern California suffers from severe air pollution, and noise and water quality conditions are beginning to approach crisis proportions. The region involving Houston is deteriorating rapidly, while many communities around San Francisco Bay are suffering similar environmental decay. It is for this reason that many inhabitants of the Pacific Northwest and British Columbia major urban regions are discouraging economic growth and the in-migration of population. They realize that rapid growth and the establishment of new industrial activities can result in environmental damage which becomes difficult to contain. Furthermore, the overconcentration of refining and metal-lurgical activities in certain regions can generate environmental impacts, such as acid rain, which may contaminate rural areas many hundreds of miles away. Environmental issues will, therefore, continue to be of considerable importance, and though in this volume the rural-urban land conversion issue has been discussed in depth, there are many others of equal importance.

A second issue that will probably become of greater importance toward the end of the 20th century is the effect of the redistribution of population on political power. Although the general settlement pattern of the continent has always resulted in a shift in political power, the relative volume of future migration streams could make the shifts quite dramatic. Furthermore, if the shifts result in some portions of the continent seeming to be burdened by a poor industrial-mix and antiquated urban infrastructure, while other regions have the advantages of new industries and urban services, then there are possibilities for sectional schisms. There have, of course, always been sectional interests in U.S. and Canadian politics, but the political implications of these have been relatively subdued. But, with greater public awareness of the interaction between government and business, and the way in which these two branches of organization can determine the location of economic opportunities, it is quite likely that regional issues will become of greater importance. The task of future governments will be to reduce friction arising from sectional rivalries, but it may well be difficult for one political party to be representative of all geographic regions in either Canada or the U.S.

Associated with the rise of sectionalism is the issue of regional stagnation. The projections of future population lead to the inescapable conclusion that areas of stagnation or decline may become more pervasive in the future unless procedures to ameliorate these conditions are introduced on a national basis. Some of the measures that may be used to ameliorate these conditions were discussed in Chapter 5. Although regional decline has been experienced in the past (such as in the coal mining areas of Appalachia and in the Canadian maritime provinces), it has not been experienced on a scale involving metropolitan areas and many millions of people. The problems arising from decline range from a lack of opportunities for the local population to social decay, and perhaps even political unrest. These are all conditions that cannot be allowed to persist on a massive scale, and evidently require political solutions. For example, there is no doubt that federal, and some state or provincial, governments could use the levers of governmental purchases and investments to influence urban development and counter these trends.[8]

With respect to the changing demands of an aging population, it is evident that the 30 million increase in population within the major urban regions by the turn of the century will permit considerable changes in the structure of urban environments. Urban growth in the recent past has been mainly in the form of suburbanization and, more recently, in decentralization to smaller towns and cities beyond the major urban regions. An aging population has a greater need for social services, health facilities, and re-creation activities, and these can be provided best in more integrated urban environments.[9] Thus, it is expected that the changes in metropolitan structure that may occur will be directed toward the creation of more communities that have both medium- and high-density residential facilities, and these facilities will need to be located in close proximity to health care and the other elements of the urban environment that are needed by an older population.

The primary lesson to be learned from the discussion of the trends and the various implications is that North American society is now far too complex to allow regional shifts, and consequent urban growth and decline, to occur without some kind of discussion of the consequences in the two countries involved. The discussion should involve not only the consequences, but whether the consequences are desirable from the point of view of (1) the various regional interests involved, (2) the impact of the trends on the availability of opportunities for the population, and (3) the general effect on the environment. It would appear to this writer that a continuation of the present trends is difficult to accept because of the inequalities in opportunity that are developing, as well as the political and environmental problems that are exacerbated. It is fairly evident that the public and private sectors, working together, can greatly influence the regional allocation of economic activity. This being so, it is time to formulate national plans for urban development which are designed to ameliorate problems arising from growth in some geographic major urban regions and stagnation or metropolitan decline in others.

NOTES

[1] U.S. Bureau of the Census, *Projections of the Population of the United States: 1977-2050* (Washington, D.C.: U.S. Department of Commerce, Series P-25, No. 704, 1977).

[2] Statistics Canada, *Population Projections for Canada and the Provinces* (Ottawa: Statistics Canada, No. 91-514, 1974).

[3] L. H. Long, *Interregional Migration of the Poor: Some Recent Changes* (Ottawa: U.S. Department of Commerce, Bureau of the Census, Current Population Reports, Series P-23, No. 73, 1978).

[4] C. L. Beale, "The Recent Shift of United States Population to Nonmetropolitan Areas, 1970-75," *International Regional Science*, Vol. 2, 2 (1977), pp. 113–122.

[5] G. Hodge and M. A. Qadeer, *Towns and Villages in Canada* (Kingston, Ont.: Queen's University), unpublished manuscript.

[6] Beale, op. cit., p. 114.

[7] Beale, op. cit., p. 118.

[8] B. L. Weinstein and R. E. Firestone, *Regional Growth and Decline in the United States: The Rise of the Sunbelt and the Decline of the Northeast* (N.Y.: Praeger, 1978).

[9] M. Yeates, "The Need for Environmental Perspectives on Issues Facing Older People" in S. Golant (ed.), *Location and Environment of Elderly Population* (Washington, D.C.: V. H. Winston & Sons, 1979).

Bibliography

Advisory Commission on Intergovernmental Relations (1977), *Trends in Metropolitan America*, Washington, D.C.: Government Printing Office.

Alonso, W. (1978), "Metropolis Without Growth," *The Public Interest, 4*, 68-86.

Alonso, W. (1973), "Urban Zero Population Growth," *Daedelus, 102,* 4, 191-206.

Alonso, W. (1971), "The Economics of Urban Size," *Papers and Proceedings of the Regional Science Association, 26,* 67-83.

Angel, W. D. (1977), "To Make a City: Entrepreneurship on the Sunbelt Frontier" in D. C. Perry and A. J. Watkins (eds.), *The Rise of the Sunbelt Cities,* Beverly Hills: Sage Publications, Urban Affairs Annual Reviews, *14,* 109-128.

Ashton, P. J. (1978), "The Political Economy of Suburban Development" in W. K. Tabb and L. Sawers (eds.), *Marxism and the Metropolis,* New York: Oxford University Press.

Baubien, C. and R. Tabacnik (1977), *People and Agricultural Land,* Ottawa: Science Council of Canada.

Beale, C. L. (1977), "The Recent Shift of United States Population to Nonmetropolitan Areas, 1970-75," *International Regional Science Review, 2,* 2, 113-122.

Beaton, W. P. and J. L. Cox (1977), "Toward an Accidental Urbanization Policy," *Journal of the American Institute of Planners,* Jan., 54-61.

Berry, B. J. L. (1970), "The Geography of the United States in the Year 2000," *Transactions of the Institute of British Geographers, 51,* 21-54.

Berry, B. J. L. and D. C. Dahmann (1977), "Population Redistribution in the United States in the 1970s," *Population and Development Review, 3,* 4, 443-471.

Berry, B. J. L. and Q. Gillard (1977), *The Changing Shape of Metropolitan America 1960-70,* Cambridge, Mass.: Ballinger.

Berry, B. J. L. and J. D. Kasarda (1977), *Contemporary Urban Ecology*, New York: Macmillan.

Bettison, D. G. (1975), *The Politics of Canadian Urban Development*, Edmonton: University of Alberta Press.

Borchert, J. R. (1972), "America's Changing Metropolitan Regions," *Annals of the American Association of Geographers, 62,* 2, 352-373.

Bourne, L. S. (1977-78), "Some Myths of Canadian Urbanization: Reflections on the 1976 Census and Beyond," *Urbanism Past and Present, 5,* 1-11.

Browning, C. E. (ed.) (1974), *Population and Urbanized Area Growth in Megalopolis*, Chapel Hill: University of North Carolina, Department of Geography.

Bureau of Municipal Research (1972), "Reorganizing Local Government: A Brief Look at Four Provinces," *Civic Affairs*, complete edition.

Cannon, J. (1975), "Government Impact on Industrial Location" in L. Collins and D. F. Walker (eds.) *Locational Dynamics of Manufacturing Activity*, New York: John Wiley & Sons.

Carey, G. (1976), "Land Tenure, Speculation, and the State of the Aging Metropolis," *Geographical Review, 66,* 253-265.

Cohen, R. B. (1977), "Multinational Corporations, International Finance, and the Sunbelt" in D. C. Perry and A. J. Watkins (eds.), *The Rise of the Sunbelt Cities*, Beverly Hills, Ca.: Sage Publications, Urban Affairs Annual Reviews, *14.*

Corbett, J. C. (1978), "Canadian Cities: How 'American' Are They?" *Urban Affairs Quarterly, 13,* 3, 383-394.

Cox, K. (ed.) (1977), *Urbanization and Conflict in Market Societies*, Chicago: Maaroufa.

Dill, H. W., Jr. and R. C. Otte (1971), *Urbanization of Land in the Northeastern United States*, Washington, D.C.: U.S. Department of Agriculture, ERS Report No. 485.

Doxiadis, C. A. (1970), *Emergence and Growth of an Urban Region*, Detroit: Detroit Edison Co.

Erickson, R. A. (1974), "The Regional Impact of Growth Firms: The Case of Boeing, 1963-68," *Land Economics, 50,* 127-136.

Friedman, J. (1973), "The Urban Field as Human Habitat" in S. P. Snow (ed.), *The Place of Planning*, Auburn, Ala.: Auburn University.

Fuchs, V. R. (1962), *Changes in the Location of Manufacturing in the United States Since 1929,* New Haven: Yale University Press.

Gans, H. J. (1962), "Urbanism and Suburbanism as Ways of Life: A Re-evaluation of Definitions" in A. Rose (ed.), *Human Behavior and Social Processes,* Boston: Houghton-Mifflin, 625-648.

Gibson, E. M. (1976), "The Urbanization of the Strait of Georgia Region," Ottawa: Environment Canada, Geography Paper No. 57.

Gierman, D. (1977), *Rural to Urban Land Conversion*, Ottawa: Lands Directorate, Fisheries and Environment.

Gilbert, A. (1976), "The Arguments for Very Large Cities Reconsidered," *Urban Studies, 13,* 27-34.

Golant, S. M. (ed.) (1979), *Location and Environment of Elderly Population*, Washington, D.C.: V. H. Winston & Sons.

Gordon, D. M. (1978), "Capitalist Development and the History of American Cities" in W. K. Tabb and L. Sawers (eds.), *Marxism and the Metropolis*, New York: Oxford University Press, 25-63.

Gordon, D. M. (1977), "Class Struggle and the Stages of American Urban Development" in D. C. Perry and A. J. Watkins (eds.), *The Rise of the Sunbelt Cities*, Beverly Hills, Ca.: Sage Publications, Urban Affairs Annual Reviews, *14*, 55-82.

Gottmann, J. (1976), "Megalopolitan Systems Around the World," *Ekistics, 243*, 109-113.

Gottman, J. (1961), *Megalopolis*, New York: Twentieth Century Fund.

Hallman, H. W. (1977), *Small and Large Together: Governing the Metropolis*, Beverly Hills: Sage Publications.

Hardwick, W. G. (1974), *Vancouver*, Don Mills: Collier-Macmillan.

Hart, J. F. (1976), "Urban Encroachment in Rural Areas," *Geographical Review, 66*, 1-17.

Hartshorn, T. A. (1976), *Metropolis in Georgia: Atlanta's Rise as a Major Transaction Center*, Cambridge, Mass.: Ballinger.

Harvey, D. (1975), "The Geography of Accumulation," *Antipode, 7*, 2, 9-21.

Harvey, D. (1975), "The Political Economy of Urbanization in Advanced Capitalist Societies: The Case of the United States" in S. Gappert and H. Rose (eds.), *The Social Economy of Cities*, Beverly Hills: Sage Publications, Urban Affairs Annual Reviews, *9*, 119-163.

Harvey, D. (1973), *Social Justice and the City*, Baltimore: Johns Hopkins Press.

Hodge, G. and M. A. Qadeer (1977), *Towns and Villages in Canada*, Kingston, Ont.: Queen's University, unpublished manuscript.

Kondratieff, N. D. (1935), "The Long Wave in Economic Life," *Review of Economics and Statistics, 17*, 105-155.

Krueger, R. R. (1978), "Urbanization of the Niagara Fruit Belt," *The Canadian Geographer, 22*, 3, 179-194.

Lande, P. S. and P. Gordon (1977), "Regional Growth in the United States: A Reexamination of the Neoclassical Model," *Journal of Regional Science, 17*, 1, 61-69.

Lantis, D. W., R. Steiner and A. E. Karinen (1977), *California: Land of Contrasts*, Dubuque, Iowa: Kendall/Hunt.

Leman, A. B. and I. A. Leman (1976), *Great Lakes Megalopolis: From Civilization to Ecumenization*, Ottawa: Supply and Services.

Long, L. H. (1978), *Interregional Migration of the Poor: Some Recent Changes*, Ottawa: U.S. Department of Commerce, Bureau of the Census, Current Population Reports, Series P-23, No. 73.

Lonsdale, R. E. and C. E. Browning (1971), "Rural-Urban Locational Preferences for Southern Manufacturers," *Annals of the Association of American Geographers, 61*, 255-268.

Lupsha, P. A. and W. J. Siembieda (1977), "The Poverty of Public Services in the Land of Plenty: An Analysis and Interpretation" in D. C. Perry and A. J. Watkins (eds.), *The Rise of the Sunbelt Cities*, Beverly Hills: Sage Publications, Urban Affairs Annual Reviews, *14*.

Markusen, A. R. and J. Fastrup (1978), "The Regional War for Federal Aid," *The Public Interest, 4,* 87-99.

Marx, K. and F. Engels (1975), *Collected Works Vols. 1-9,* New York: International Publishers. These are reprints of the writings of Marx and Engels published originally in a variety of places during the 1840s.

McDowell, B. D. (ed.) (1974), *A Look to the North: Canadian Regional Experience,* Advisory Commission on Intergovernmental Relations.

Mercer, J. and J. Hultquist (1976), "National Progress Toward Housing and Urban Renewal Goals," in J. S. Adams (ed.), *Urban Policymaking and Metropolitan Dynamics,* Cambridge, Mass.: Ballinger.

Mills, E. S. (1972), "Welfare Aspects of National Policy Toward City Sizes," *Urban Studies, 9,* 1, 117-128.

Moriarty, B. M. (1978), "A Note on Unexplained Residuals in North-South Wage Differentials," *Journal of Regional Science, 18,* 1, 105-108.

Morrison, P. A. (1977), "Current Demographic Changes in Regions of the United States," Santa Monica, Ca.: The Rand Corporation, P-6000.

Morrison, P. A. (1977), "Emerging Public Concerns over U.S. Population Movements in an Era of Slowing Growth," Santa Monica, Ca.: The Rand Corporation, P-5873.

Moynihan, D. P. (1978), "The Politics and Economics of Regional Growth," *The Public Interest, 51,* Spring, 3-21.

Nader, G. A. (1976), *Cities of Canada, Vol. 2: Profiles of Fifteen Metropolitan Centres,* Toronto: Macmillan of Canada.

Nader, G. A. (1975), *Cities of Canada, Vol. 1: Theoretical, Historical and Planning Perspectives,* Toronto: Macmillan of Canada.

Nourse, H. O. (1978), "Equivalence of Central Place and Economic Base Theories of Urban Growth," *Journal of Urban Economics, 5,* 543-549.

Otte, R. C. (1974), *Farming in the City's Shadow, Urbanization of Land and Changes in Farm Output in Standard Metropolitan Statistical Areas, 1960-70,* Washington, D.C.: U.S. Department of Agriculture, ERS Report No. 250.

Palmer, M. E. and M. N. Rush (1976), "Houston" in J. Adams (ed.), *Contemporary Metropolitan America: Twentieth Century Cities,* Cambridge, Mass.: Ballinger, 107-149.

Perry, D. C. and A. J. Watkins (eds.) (1977), *The Rise of the Sunbelt Cities,* Beverly Hills: Sage Publications, Urban Affairs Annual Reviews, *14.*

Perry, D. C. and A. J. Watkins (1977), "Regional Change and the Impact of Uneven Urban Development" in D. C. Perry and A. J. Watkins (eds.), *The Rise of the Sunbelt Cities,* Beverly Hills, Ca.: Sage Publications, Urban Affairs Annual Reviews, *14.*

Peterson, G. and T. Muller (1979), "The Regional Impact of Federal Tax and Spending Policies" in *Alternatives to Confrontation: A National Policy Toward Economic Development,* Lexington: Saxon House/Lexington Books (forthcoming).

Pred, A. (1965), "Industrialization, Initial Advantage, and American Metropolitan Growth," *Geographical Review, 55,* 158-185.

Pred, A. R. (1974), *Major Job-Providing Organizations and Systems of Cities*, Washington, D.C.: American Association of Geographers, Resource Paper No. 27.

Radburn, S. (1977-78), "Responding to the Decline of Industrial America," *Urbanism Past and Present, 5,* 37-42.

Ray, D. M. (ed.) (1976), *Canadian Urban Trends: Metropolitan Perspectives, Vol. II,* Toronto: Copp-Clark.

Richardson, H. W. (1973), *The Economics of Urban Size,* Lexington: Saxon House/ Lexington Books.

Rostow, W. W. (1977), "Regional Change in the Fifth Kondratieff Upswing" in D. C. Perry and A. J. Watkins (eds.), *The Rise of the Sunbelt Cities,* Beverly Hills, Ca.: Sage Publications, Urban Affairs Annual Reviews, *14.*

Russwurm, L. H. (1977), *The Surroundings of Our Cities: Problems and Planning Implications of Urban Fringe Landscapes,* Ottawa: Community Planning Press.

Russwurm, L. H. (1970), *Development of an Urban Corridor System: Toronto to Stratford Area, 1941-1966,* Toronto: Queen's Printer.

Rust, E. (1975), *No Growth Impacts on Metropolitan Areas,* Lexington, Mass.: D. C. Heath.

Simmons, J. W. (1978), "Migration and the Canadian Urban System: Part II, Simple Realtionships," Toronto: Centre for Urban and Community Studies, University of Toronto, Res. Paper No. 98.

Simpson, J. K. and M. Cromie (1977), *Where Canadians Work,* Ottawa: Statistics Canada, 99-719.

Statistics Canada (1974), *Population Projections for Canada and the Provinces,* Ottawa: Statistics Canada, No. 91-514.

Sternleib, G. and J. W. Hughes (1977), "New Regional and Metropolitan Realities of America," *Journal of the American Institute of Planners,* July, 227-234.

Stone, L. O. and C. Marceau (1977), *Canadian Population Trends and Public Policy Through the 1980's,* Montreal: McGill–Queen's University Press and I.R.P.P.

Swatridge, L. A. (1971), *The Bosnywash Megalopolis: A Region of Great Cities,* New York: McGraw-Hill.

Tabb, W. K. (1978), "The New York City Fiscal Crisis" in W. K. Tabb and L. Sawers (eds.), *Marxism and the Metropolis,* N.Y.: Oxford University Press, 241-266.

U.S. Bureau of the Census (1977), *Projections of the Population of the United States: 1977-2050,* Washington, D.C.: U.S. Department of Commerce, Series P-25, No. 704.

Wade, R. (1976--77), "The End of the Self-Sufficient City: New York's Fiscal Crisis in History," *Urbanism Past and Present,* winter, 1-4.

Walker, R. A. (1979), "A Theory of Suburbanization: Capitalism and the Construction of Urban Space in the United States" in M. Dear and A. Scott (eds.), *Urbanization and Urban Planning,* Chicago: Maaroufa Press.

Walker, R. A. (1977), "The Transformation of Urban Structure in the Nineteenth Century and the Beginnings of Suburbanization" in K. Cox (ed.), *Urbanization and Conflict in Market Societies,* Chicago: Maaroufa Press, 165-212.

Weinstein, B. L. and R. E. Firestone (1978), *Regional Growth and Decline in the United States: The Rise of the Sunbelt and the Decline of the Northeast*, New York: Praeger.

Wheat, L. F. (1976), *Urban Growth in the Non-Metropolitan South*, Farnborough, Hants.: Lexington Books.

Wirth, L. (1938), "Urbanism as a Way of Life," *American Journal of Sociology, 44*, July, 3-24.

Yeates, M. (1979), "The Need for Environmental Perspectives on Issues Facing Older People" in S. Golant (ed.), *Location and Environment of Elderly Population*, Washington, D.C.: V. H. Winston & Sons.

Yeates, M. (1978), "The Future Urban Requirements of Canada's Elderly," *Plan Canada, 18*, 2, 88-104.

Yeates, M. (1975), *Main Street: Windsor to Quebec City*, Toronto: Macmillan of Canada.

Yeates, M. and B. Garner (1980), *The North American City* (3rd ed.), N.Y.: Harper & Row.

Yezer, A. M. J. and R. S. Goldfarb (1978), "An Indirect Test of Efficient City Sizes," *Journal of Urban Economics, 15*, 46-65.

Zeimetz, K. A. et al. (1976), *Dynamics of Land Use in Fast Growth Areas*, Washington, D.C.: USDA, A. E. Report 325.

Zelinsky, W. (1977), "The Pennsylvania Town: An Overdue Geographical Account," *Geographical Review, 67*, 2, 127-147.

Index